GETTIN' OLD
AIN'T FOR WIMPS
VOLUME 2

KAREN O'CONNOR

HARVEST HOUSE PUBLISHERS
EUGENE, OREGON

All Scripture quotations are taken from the Holy Bible, New International Version®, NIV®. Copyright © 1973, 1978, 1984, 2011 by Biblica, Inc.® Used by permission of Zondervan. All rights reserved worldwide. www.zondervan.com. The "NIV" and "New International Version" are trademarks registered in the United States Patent and Trademark Office by Biblica, Inc.®

Verses marked KJV are taken from King James Version of the Bible.

Names and minor details have been changed in the real-life stories shared in this book to protect the privacy of the individuals mentioned.

Cover design by Dugan Design Group

Interior design by Chad Dougherty

For bulk, special sales, or ministry purchases, please call 1-800-547-8979.
Email: Customerservice@hhpbooks.com

M This logo is a federally registered trademark of the Hawkins Children's LLC. Harvest House Publishers, Inc., is the exclusive licensee of this trademark.

Compilation of the best stories from *The Golden Years Ain't for Wimps* (978-0-7369-2247-0), *Walkin' with God Ain't for Wimps* (978-0-7369-2038-4), and *It's Taken Years to Get This Old* (978-0-7369-2953-0).

Gettin' Old Ain't for Wimps Volume 2
Copyright © 2006, 2007, 2008 by Karen O'Connor
Published by Harvest House Publishers
Eugene, Oregon 97408
www.harvesthousepublishers.com

ISBN 978-0-7369-8476-8 (pbk.)
ISBN 978-0-7369-8477-5 (eBook)

Library of Congress Cataloging-in-Publication Data is on file at the Library of Congress, Washington, DC

Printed in the United States of America
22 23 24 25 26 27 28 29 30 / BP / 10 9 8 7 6 5 4 3 2 1

To June

My sister waiting for me on the other side

Contents

Part 5: Those Grandkids

Part 6: Aging Parents

Part 7: Old Dog, New Tricks

Part 8: Body Works

A Note from the Author

Oh those golden years! There are times when they glitter and times when they're a bit lackluster. Health problems, financial concerns, and relationship challenges can tarnish an otherwise happy day. On the other hand, we're generally confident in who we are, know how to enjoy life, have children and grandchildren to keep us young, and are wise enough to laugh at our foibles!

I hope you'll enjoy this collection of original, lighthearted stories and inspirations to warm your heart and tickle your funny bone. Included are scriptures and prayers to nurture your spirit and turn your eyes to the One who made us, who numbered our days, and who promises clearly that he will never leave us nor forsake us—right up to our last breath…and beyond.

Let us hold unswervingly to the hope we profess,
for he who promised is faithful.
HEBREWS 10:23

—Karen O'Connor

PART 1

WHAT'S IN
A WORD?

The Exhausted King

⌒⟨⊙⟩⌒

Harvey had gotten hearing aids, but he doubted they were doing their job. His wife tugged on his shirtsleeve and whispered in his ear more often than he wanted to admit. It seemed he was confusing words, mishearing initial sounds, and generally "missing the boat," especially when there were more than three or four people talking. About the only place he felt confident was in the first row of St. Andrew's Presbyterian Church, where he'd been a faithful member for more than 50 years.

But there was another problem—one Harvey was equally bummed about. He had a difficult time staying awake during Pastor Richard's sermons. He wished he could sit in the back so the minister wouldn't notice, but if he did he couldn't hear as well. On the other hand, if he snoozed he'd miss part of the sermon anyway—so what difference did it make where he sat? Harvey had a dilemma. He decided to put off his decision and spend the next few weeks sitting on the side near the worship group.

The following Sunday Harvey and Mabel arrived ten minutes before the service began. They chose two seats on the right side. Leonard Fuchs, the choir director, came into the sanctuary and took his place in front of the singers. Harvey leaned back and allowed the music to waft over him, filling his spirit with peace and joy and the love of the Lord.

He felt so good that he didn't care what happened next. He was already in ecstasy. He felt himself nod off a couple of times, but he pulled himself back to reality when the music swelled.

After the service he and Mabel walked out to the vestibule, greeted their friends, shook hands with Pastor Richard, and strolled out to their car in the corner of the parking lot.

Harvey tucked his hand in Mabel's and gave it a playful squeeze. "I loved the music today, didn't you? I felt as though I were sleeping on a cloud."

"It wasn't a cloud, dear. It was a seat—in church. And you not only snoozed, you snored. So I'm surprised you even heard the music at all."

Harvey dropped his wife's hand. "Not true," he growled. "I heard every word. I even know the title. It was my favorite song."

Mabel looked at him out of the side of her eyes. "And what might that title be?" she asked with a bite in her voice.

"'The King Is Exhausted on High.' So there!"

Mabel breathed deeply. "The correct title, dear, is 'The King Is Exalted on High,' not 'Exhausted.' You're the one who was exhausted, Harvey, not the Lord."

Reflection

Come to me, all you who are weary and burdened,
and I will give you rest (Matthew 11:28).

———————

Lord, I don't know about you, but I feel exhausted sometimes—mostly of my own doing. I take on too much, worry too much, and meddle too much. It's time for me to take a break from other people's business, and my own too, and just focus my attention on you, the author and finisher of all things.

Green Jell-O

❧

"Y ou lying piece of green Jell-O!" Raymond bellowed across the room to his wife, Paulette.

"What did you say?" Paulette barked, clearly insulted and confused. Raymond looked at his wife like she'd lost her mind. Paulette popped off the sofa and ran out of the den in tears.

"What brought that on?" she asked God. "Is this it? Raymond is finally losing his mind? I know he's hard of hearing, but this is too much. What if he becomes dangerous?"

Paulette remembered having read about a man who chased his wife of 60 years out of the house with a butcher knife. He had been failing mentally for months, but then he became violent and she had to move him to a home for people with dementia. Paulette's thoughts raced on. Within seconds she was already planning what she'd tell their children and how their entire life would be turned upside down if Raymond were seriously mentally ill.

Paulette walked back to the den and stood in the door-way, ready to bolt if her husband lunged at her. She eyed him suspiciously. She knew it would only make matters worse if she got upset in front of him, so she controlled herself and asked him to repeat what he said. That would give her a chance to judge his mental state and decide what to do if he repeated the same phrase.

"You're lying on the cream pillow," he restated slowly in a loud voice.

Paulette burst out laughing. She and Raymond had agreed they would not rest their heads on the new cream-colored decorative pillows they'd bought for their sofa because they didn't want to stain them. Raymond was simply reminding her.

When she told him she thought he had called her a "lying piece of green Jell-O," he nearly fell off his chair laughing.

"After that my heart calmed down, and I let go of my fantasy of nursing homes and butcher knives," said Paulette.

"I'm not the only one around here who's hard of hearing!" exclaimed Raymond. "Looks like our next stop is the hearing aid center. I wonder if they have a two-for-one sale?"

Reflection

Let me hear joy and gladness (Psalm 51:8).

———————————

Lord, thank you that even when I cannot hear you, you hear me and my cry for help. I pray today for the spiritual ears to hear your teachings and to apply them to my life.

Cracking the Code

ᕙᕤᕚᕤᕙᕤ

L yle, dear, I can't find the thingamajig that goes with the what-chamacallit. Any idea where you put it?"

Lyle walked into the guest bathroom, scratching his head. "The thingamajig? What the heck is that?"

Ellie's look pinned her husband to the tile wall. "What do you mean you don't know? You're the one who had it last."

Lyle crossed his arms in front of his chest. "Did not."

Ellie crossed hers. "Did too." She took a breath and stretched out her words. "Let me start over. You know," she continued, uncrossing her arms and flailing them in front of Lyle's face, "you came in from that store—you know that whozywhatsit place where you bought the whateveryoucallit thingy for this bathroom. Renae called this morning. She wants to buy one just like it. I told her I'd ask you the price and if there was a choice of color." Ellie stood her ground and didn't flinch.

"Look, dear, I can't help you if I don't know what you're talking about. I bought a bunch of supplies at the diddleywhatsit place, and then I stopped by the—you know the store that makes me think of trains."

Ellie blinked and knitted her brows. "The place that makes you think of trains?"

"Hmmm." Lyle appeared determined to save face. He raised his voice. "It's a store that sells stuff for people that like to do—you know—projects, stuff that helps with gardening and plumbing and lighting and painting."

"And that kind of a store reminds you of trains? Do they sell miniature train sets?"

"No!" Lyle's face turned red. "They don't sell trains. It just reminds me of trains. You know, the place where a train goes after it's finished with its run."

"A train garage?" Ellie decided to try and help her husband, but she hadn't a clue where all this was leading.

"Warm, but not hot," said Lyle, egging her on with his fingers. "Keep going. You're almost there."

"What is this—a treasure hunt?" Ellie fanned her face with a hand. She had no idea how they got into this corner. There seemed to be no way out. "A train shed?"

"No, but you're getting there, I think."

"A depot—a train depot!"

"That's it!" Lyle crushed Ellie to his chest. "You're a genius. Now I can get a good night's sleep."

"But it's only ten in the morning." Ellie collapsed in her recliner. She had forgotten how all this started, and it didn't matter anymore. Her husband needed her. He was clearly on the precipice of a mental breakdown.

Lyle threw up his hands. "Home Depot!" he shouted. "Get it? Depot!"

Ellie sighed. She was relieved, but not amused. Lyle would be okay—at least for the moment.

"Now, back to our initial conversation," she said, lips pursed. "The one about that thingamajig that goes with the whatchama-callit. Any idea where you put it?"

"Not a clue, but if we go back to the Depot and walk up and down the aisles I'm sure we'll find what we're looking for. It's bound to be there somewhere. If it has to do with bathrooms, we'll check every doodad in every aisle until we find the hottle-dee-hoo. What do you say?"

"I say let's go. The train is waiting."

Reflection

Forget the former things; do not dwell
on the past (Isaiah 43:18).

———————

Lord, thank you that even my whodlewhatsit prayers make sense to you. You are never confused by my conversations. I am so relieved to know that the Holy Spirit intercedes for me when I can't find the words I want to say.

`Hear! Hear!

∽✺✺∾

Say that again."

"Didn't get it."

"Speak up."

It got so bad around the Jones' household that Maggie couldn't stand it another minute. "Conner, you've got to get hearing aids. This dilemma is interfering with our marriage. I can't spend the next decade repeating everything I say. I'll go insane! Do you hear me? Oh nuts! You can't hear me. That's the problem."

Maggie wrung her hands and walked into the kitchen. She pulled out sugar and flour and butter and pecans and a baking pan. She turned on the oven, tied an apron around her middle, and opened her cookbook. She'd do what she always did when she and Conner were at a crossroads: Bake! A pie, some cookies, a dozen cupcakes made her feel better.

The doorbell rang just as she set her first batch of goodies on the granite counter to cool. Their neighbors Abby and Ray had stopped by to say hi.

"Come in. You're just in time to enjoy a slice of pie and some butter pecan cookies. How about some coffee or a cup of tea?" Maggie turned toward Conner sitting in his favorite chair with the TV blaring. "Honey," she shouted, "look who's here."

"What? Say it again!"

Maggie let out a deep breath. She turned to their friends. "See what I mean? It's getting worse by the day, and he doesn't seem to realize it."

Ray walked over and patted Conner on the shoulder. "We're here to visit. Come join us."

Conner stood up and smiled. He pumped Ray's hand and welcomed Abby too.

The four sat down for dessert.

Ray opened the conversation. "Con, Maggie tells us you're thinking about getting hearing aids. Good idea. I'll be looking into them in a few years myself." He laughed and looked around for approval.

Conner sat with a straight face. "I don't know what you're talking about. I'm fine. Can hear as good as anyone."

Ray backed down and then took a new direction. "I agree. Why would you need those things anyway? They're a nuisance, and they cost an arm and a leg. Besides, why would any man want hearing aids? If you stay hard of hearing you won't have to listen to your wife. Hardy-har-har." He thought it was funny. Abby and Maggie did not.

Conner saved the day. "I'd never stay hard of hearing for that reason," he said. "I'd miss hearing Maggie say, 'I love you,' just before we drop off to sleep. Funny how I never miss that one— no matter what."

Reflection

Hear my cry, O God; listen to my prayer
(Psalm 61:1).

Thank you, Lord, for hearing my every word and for speaking to me in such a way that I can hear every word you say.

Spell It Again, Sam

orey walked up and down the aisles of the supermarket, selecting one item after another. A box of cereal. A bottle of apple juice. A dozen eggs. Two cans of cream of mushroom soup. A couple of ripe tomatoes and a sack of Idaho potatoes. "That should do it," she muttered to herself. As she passed by the freezer foods, she caught her reflection in the glass doors, then gasped. "Lord, I hope I don't run into anyone I know! I can't get by in public anymore without makeup. I really should take time to look nice before leaving the house!"

So far so good, she thought as she wheeled the cart to the checkout stand and unloaded her groceries onto the conveyor. Two check stands over, she spotted a familiar face. *Janice, no Jody... or is it Jean? That doesn't sound right either. What is her name? If I could think of her last name, I'm sure her first name would pop up. Here I go again. Names are dropping from my mind as fast as leaves from a tree in autumn.*

Corey didn't want to embarrass herself, especially considering the way she looked in her painter's shorts and faded T-shirt and with her hair pushed on top of her head with a clip that didn't quite do the job.

I'll look the other way. Hey, there's nothing to worry about. She won't recognize me in this get-up. I'll pay and go—fast. Corey was pleased with her plan.

"Corey, hi! I thought it was you I spotted." The woman hurried over and reached out for a hug. "It's been a couple of years at least. Do you live around here?"

God, please, what is her name? I'd rather die than admit I don't know it. Look at how friendly she is. How embarrassing to have to ask her name.

"So what's new with you and Gene?" the woman probed as Corey handed the clerk her charge card and then signed the receipt.

She not only remembers me, but my husband too? Oh great. This is getting worse by the minute.

"Gene. Yes, Gene's fine. And you and your family?" *I don't remember if she's married or has children. This is awful.*

Corey pushed her basket through the stand and headed for the door, turning to the woman, while still fishing for her name.

"I'm alone now," the woman said. "Skip died last year. It's been quite an adjustment."

"I'm sorry…" Corey said, uncertain about what to say next.

"Maybe we can get together," the woman said. "I'm doing my best to reconnect with old friends. It's a blessing to run into you."

Corey felt her palms grow wet and her heart race. She gathered all the courage she could muster. "Help me out, will you? I seem to remember…" Corey lost her nerve. She just couldn't admit that she had forgotten the woman's name. "As I recall," she stammered, "your name has an unusual spelling. Would you mind telling me again? I want to get it right once and for all."

"Jill. J-I-L-L. Jones. J-O-N-E-S."

And now for my next act! Corey said to herself as she cringed.

Reflection

Those who complain will accept instruction
(Isaiah 29:24).

———————

Dear God, my "rememberer" isn't working too well these days, especially with names from the past. I need some help. Mostly I need your grace to give up being too proud to ask for help when I need it. There's no shame in forgetting. But there is shame in not acknowledging that I'm human and can use a bit of assistance from time to time.

PART 2

SENIOR MOMENTS

Here Yesterday, Gone Today

C harles, have you seen my white cotton sun hat?"

"No. Where'd you have it last?"

Such questions were becoming routine in our household. If Charles wasn't asking me the whereabouts of his sunglasses, I was asking him where I put a certain pair of socks or a pillow or now my favorite sun hat. This had never been the case with me before...before I turned 60, that is, but now that I'm pushing 70—and pushing it hard—I'm noticing I'm becoming a bit more distracted. Okay, downright forgetful.

I thought about where I'd last seen the hat. I'd worn it on a walk with a friend one morning. After that Charles and I went grocery shopping and then out for lunch. I remembered having the hat with me in the market and at the restaurant. After that—nothing. A dead end.

The search continued for weeks until I'd exhausted every possible spot in our home and cars. I could only assume I'd laid it down on the bench in the restaurant and gone off without it. I checked with the manager, but he hadn't seen it. So either I didn't leave it there *or* someone took off with it.

C'est la vie. I had to let it go. Twice I came across other white hats in boutiques and shops we visited, but none could compare to the one I misplaced—in style, comfort, or price. I wore an old one I didn't like very much and told myself I'd have to "make do" since I was responsible for the loss.

I did ask the Lord to lead me to my missing hat, if it was within my grasp. And I mentioned that I'd love to take it with me on our next vacation. We were to leave in a week. God heard me and delivered quickly. He knew I was running short on time! I took my suitcase down from the closet shelf a couple of days later so I could begin packing a few things at a time. I opened a zippered section that I rarely use to see what I might fit in that compartment for the upcoming trip. *This is a good spot for a floppy hat or a paperback book,* I thought as I reached inside.

What's this? I had left something behind the last time I used the bag. There it was! My soft, white, floppy hat! I suddenly remembered I'd taken it on my last trip.

I pulled my hat out and hugged it as tightly as I might a long-lost friend. In a way it was exactly that. I was so excited! I put it on immediately and invited my husband to go for a walk with me.

"On one condition," he said with a wrinkled brow.

"And that is?"

"That when we get back you put it in the closet with our other hats—where it belongs—until we pack for our trip. Then you'll know where to find it."

I smooched him good and agreed. Then we went for our stroll—I in my newly found sun hat and he in his favorite ball cap.

Reflection

The Lord is not slow in keeping his promise
(2 Peter 3:9).

Dear God, I could open a clothing shop with all the clothes and accessories I've lost and found and then lost again over the past few months. I feel like an absent-minded professor! Help me be more careful and mindful of what I'm doing.

Fast Getaway

ᶜᵍᵒ

Reena regretted that she never learned to drive, but at age 71 she wasn't about to take lessons. In one way she missed the independence that driving brings, but in another way she enjoyed having others drive her to the store, to doctors' appointments, and so on.

One Saturday morning her daughter's husband stopped by to fix a leaking pipe. While he was there, Reena asked if he'd mind driving her to the grocery store so she could stock up for the weekend.

"Be glad to," he said, "as soon as I'm finished."

An hour later the two were on their way, Brad behind the wheel of his pickup and Reena in the passenger seat, grocery list in hand.

He pulled into the parking lot of Shop 'n Save and Reena slid out. "Give me 20 minutes," she said. "I don't want to hold you up."

"No problem," Brad said. "I'll just put my head back and listen to the radio. Take your time."

Reena rushed around the market, plopping one item after

another into her grocery cart. There was a long line at the check-out lane, and she worried about keeping Brad away from home too long.

Finally it was her turn. The checker rang up her items, Reena paid, and then hurried out the door. She rushed through the parking lot as quickly as she could while steering the cart with wobbly wheels. "Just my luck to get *this* one," she moaned.

She stopped for a moment to be sure she was going down the correct aisle. Then she spotted the white pickup and headed right to it. Reena plopped her bag into the cab in back and jumped in the passenger seat. She fastened the seat belt and turned to the driver. "Okay. Mission accomplished. Let's get out of here…oh my gosh, you're not Brad! Who are you?"

A huge grin broke across the driver's face. "I was going to ask you the same question! Where to? Sounds like you have something fun planned."

Reena was suddenly hot all over. She grabbed the door handle and popped out. "I'm so sorry," she called through the window. "Your truck looks just like my son-in-law's."

Just then Brad pulled up, laughing so hard he could hardly contain himself. "Going my way?" he shouted.

Reena reached for her bag of groceries, hoisted it out of the other man's cab, and held it tight as she slid into Brad's truck. Off they went, laughing all the way home.

Reflection

Then you will lift up your face without shame;
you will stand firm and without fear (Job 11:15).

———————

Lord, these senior moments are becoming more and more embarrassing. I'm grateful I can hold up my head with you no matter what I do.

Nice Game

❧ ᘓ ᘓ ❧

Nora and Larry were proud of their grandson, Phil. He had made the college basketball team, as did his childhood friend, Roy. Nora looked forward to attending the playoffs with both young men on the court.

"I wanted to make a good impression on Phil and his friends, to show them that I was a hip grandma, still attractive for my age, and that I knew a thing or two about athletics," said Nora.

So she spent the afternoon before the game in the hair salon. "I had a facial, a wash and blow dry, and a manicure and pedicure. I wore my new Calvin Klein jeans and a cute striped shirt. The only thing missing to make the look complete was a stylish pair of glasses frames. Unfortunately, my new lenses and frames wouldn't be ready till the following week, and I was not about to wear the ugly specs I was trading in. I decided I would make do. We had front-row seats and my husband would be with me, so he could fill me in on any plays too far away for me to see clearly."

As the couple drove to the game, Larry briefed Nora *again* on the nuances of basketball and reminded her of who was who on the team. He knew the numbers of all the players.

"The game was a thriller, I have to admit," Nora said later. "Phil and his team played hard and won hard! After the game, Larry and I rushed to the court with hundreds of screaming fans.

"Phil, we are so proud of you!" Nora squealed and threw her arms around her six-foot-four grandson.

His teammate Roy stood beside him. "You too, Roy," Nora said and reached up to hug him. "I'm just so proud of the two of you."

"Thanks, Grams," said Phil. Then he turned to Roy and shrugged.

Roy chuckled and hugged Nora back. "Thank you, Mrs. Johnson, but I haven't played since last year. You probably missed seeing me on the bench."

Nora's face grew hot with embarrassment! "Oh…but you played great last year," she blurted out without thinking, then excused herself to go to the ladies' room. "I needed a good splash of cold water!"

Reflection

You are my hiding place; you will protect me from trouble and surround me with songs of deliverance (Psalm 32:7).

———————

Sometimes, Lord, I embarrass myself to the point of wanting to hide! But then I remember that you are my hiding place and you will always guide me back to right thinking and behaving.

Everything in Its Place

ꙮ

"Nana, what are you looking for?" seven-year-old Matty asked his grandmother Esther as she searched under and around the cushions on the den sofa.

"I'm not sure," she said. "This seems to be happening a lot these days. I put down my glasses or my Bible or my special pen on a certain table or shelf, so I'll remember where I laid it. And then I forget which table in which room."

"I have an idea," said Matty. "Pick a room for each thing. Put your glasses in the bedroom by your bed so you'll see 'em when you wake up. And put your Bible on the kitchen table so you'll see it when you make breakfast."

"Good idea. Why didn't I think of that?" Esther ruffled the boy's curly hair. "Oh Matty, I wish it were that simple. For a seven-year-old it is 'cause your brain is young and alert."

"What's alert mean?" he asked.

"Means your brain is like a soldier standing at attention, waiting for orders."

Matty laughed and ran off to play.

Later that day Esther's daughter Carol stopped by to pick up Matty after work. Esther told her about the conversation she'd had with Matty. They both had a good laugh. Carol admitted that even at age 44 she was beginning to forget things.

"I walk into a room," she said, "then stand around wondering what I'm looking for. Sometimes I have to go back to where I started so I'll remember. Then I run to the room and grab the item before I forget again!"

The following week, Carol and Matty stopped by on Saturday. Carol was carrying a long cardboard box with her. She presented it to her mother. "Found this at a garage sale and thought it was a perfect decoration for your *bathroom* door," she said.

Puzzled, Esther opened the carton and pulled out a wooden plaque with large lettering. She read it aloud, and then exploded with laughter.

PLEASE DO NOT DISTURB
THIS IS THE ONLY ROOM
I CAN GO INTO AND NOT FORGET
WHAT I CAME IN FOR.

Reflection

You will surely forget your trouble, recalling it
only as waters gone by (Job 11:16).

———————

Lord, it's scary to forget things, especially when they are important. I remember leaving the stove on and

*forgetting to turn off the water in the bathroom, silly
stuff that can be dangerous if I don't remember on
time. But you know my weaknesses as I grow older. I'm
reminded to lean on your understanding not on mine,
and then I can relax and depend on you completely.*

Keyed Up

⁓ↄ⊙ↄ⊙ↄ⊙ↄ⊙ↄ⊙ↄ⊙

Irene hurried out of the grocery store, holding her umbrella and car key in her right hand and her sack of groceries in her left arm. She dodged puddles and nearly lost her balance as she approached her blue minivan parked in the last slot in the third aisle from the street in front of the store.

She set the grocery bag down at her feet, holding the umbrella over herself and the bag as she juggled the key into the tip of the lock. *Darn!* No response. *What is going on here? Of all times for the lock to jam.*

Irene thought about calling her husband but realized she had left her cell phone at home in the charger. One bad episode after another had happened—and on a day when she was expecting company for lunch.

She felt like collapsing on the payment and sobbing—having a real pity party! She tried the key one more time. Still the lock wouldn't budge.

Suddenly someone came up behind her. She turned at the

sound of a man's words. "Having a problem?" he asked. "Maybe I can help."

"Gee, thanks, but it seems the lock is jammed. I think I'll need a locksmith for this one. I don't understand. This has never happened before!"

The gentleman smiled and produced a key as if by magic. "Try *this* one. I promise it will work." He chuckled as Irene stood there dumbfounded.

Then he pointed to a blue minivan one aisle over facing the same direction as the van she was standing next to. "And try your key in *that* vehicle!"

Irene put a hand to her mouth and burst out laughing. "You get the fairy godfather award for the day," she quipped. "I guess this is what my friends would call a 'senior moment.' Of course this is the *first* one I've ever had!"

The two nodded goodbye. Irene went off to *her* van, and the fairy godfather got into his.

Reflection

I will forget my complaint, I will change my
expression, and smile (Job 9:27).

———————

Dear Lord, thank you for rescuing me from situations that appear overwhelming. They are nothing to you, but you never hold them over my head. You simply give me the grace I need without recrimination. How wonderful you are.

No Fries Here

❧

Callie clocked out of the store at noon. She had one hour to eat lunch, run to the bank, pick up her dry cleaning, return two phone calls, and drop off a package at the post office.

She pulled out of the parking lot and onto the busy thoroughfare. The street was jammed with cars and trucks.

How will I get all this done and have time to eat? she wondered. *Gotta try. No time for errands tomorrow or the next day.*

Callie made it into the post office ahead of a woman with a luggage carrier loaded with five extra-large boxes. She had prepaid her dry cleaning so that stop took just a minute or two. She returned the phone calls as she drove from one place to the other, though uncomfortable doing so. It was getting more difficult to do two things at once. She had turned 60 the month before and suddenly she was feeling her age. She couldn't process things as quickly as she had just a couple of years before.

Callie pulled over to the side of the road and took out her to-do list to make sure she hadn't forgotten anything. She crossed off each item she'd completed.

dry cleaning
post office
phone calls
lunch
bank deposit

Callie was suddenly starved. *I've got to eat or I'll faint.* She spotted a Best Burger Drive-Thru near the bank. *Perfect. I'll grab some food then deposit my check without having to make an extra stop.* She glanced at her watch. Twenty minutes left.

Callie prepared her deposit slip while waiting in the drive-thru lane.

"Your order, please." The voice over the intercom brought her to attention.

"Double burger without onion, fries, and a Coke. Thank you."

Callie pulled up to the window, received her bagged lunch, and handed over her payment.

"Sorry, ma'am," the clerk said with a smile. "We don't take deposit slips here, but there is a bank next door."

Callie felt her face grow warm. She took back the deposit, grabbed a bill, paid for her lunch, and drove from the burger drive-thru to the bank drive-thru. *Maybe it's time to retire and head for the rocking chair,* she thought, laughing at herself.

She pulled up to the teller at the window.

"May I help you?" the woman asked.

"Double burger without onion, fries, and a Coke….I mean…"

The teller laughed. "We don't have a lunch menu here," she joked, "but there's a Best Burger next door."

Callie joked back as she handed over her check and deposit

slip. "I should have known. Best Burger wouldn't take my deposit slip either."

Reflection

For six days, work is to be done, but the seventh
day is a Sabbath of rest, holy to the LORD
(Exodus 31:15).

---

*Lord, thank you that when I rush through life trying
to make things happen, you are there to remind me of
what is most important—taking time to rest in you.*

Running on Empty

❦

"Have a nice weekend," Lettie called to her co-workers as they got out of Cathy's car and walked to their vehicles parked in the carpool lot.

"You too, Lettie," Cathy shouted just before she hit the accelerator and drove off. Lisa and Marion waved goodbye and went to their cars.

Lettie was parked at the far end of the lot, so she had a bit of a trek, but she didn't mind. "It felt good to move my legs and breathe the fresh air. As I got closer to the fence," she said, "I heard what I thought was an engine running. I thought that was odd because my car was the only one left in the area."

Then Lettie suddenly realized it *was* her car. *Oh no!* It had idled for nearly 12 hours, including travel time to and from Ohio State University, where all the women taught school.

"I stood there for a moment looking at my van as though an alien had descended on it," she said laughing. "The next thing I knew Marion and Lisa were beside me in their vehicles, asking if I needed help.

"I guess so," I said. "I feel a bit stupid. I forgot to shut off the motor this morning. Can you believe it?" Then Lettie issued a stern warning. "Don't you dare breathe a word of this to my students, you rascals. They think I'm smart. I have a Ph.D.!"

The women roared as Lettie slid into the driver's seat and checked the fuel gauge. "Thankfully I filled my tank last night," she called out the window. "I think I have just enough to make it to the service station at the corner."

"Maybe one of us should follow you," said Lisa, "just in case..."

Lettie finished her sentence for her. "In case the old girl has lost all her marbles, leaves the car at the station, engine running, and then walks home! Okay, I'll take you up on it."

Lisa and Marion followed Lettie to the station. She filled her tank, then bought each of the gals a large soda. They stood in the driveway, clicked cans, and toasted the onset of mental-pause!

Reflection

My help comes from the LORD, the Maker of
heaven and earth (Psalm 121:2).

How embarrassing to do something so contrary to my usual behavior. I'm shocked at some of the stunts I pull, O Lord. But you're not. You know I'm just a human being with all the failings and flaws that go with it. I'm so thankful that I can rely on you to help me work things out and recover my confidence.

Couch Potato

Millie and Ron decided to run errands on Tuesday morning. They each had a gift certificate for a haircut from their neighbor Jan, a hairdresser. After leaving that shop they spotted Save-a-Lot across the street, where everything in the store is discounted. They walked over and went in. Millie went up one aisle with the shopping cart while Ron went down another with a basket. She gathered boxes of crackers and cookies. Ron loaded up on cherry soda and his favorite brand of potato chips—the one that earned him the nickname "couch potato" from Millie. He chuckled as he picked up three bags. He did love to munch chips and drink cherry soda while sitting on the sofa watching TV.

The two met in the back of the store and decided the sale price on paper goods was worth taking advantage of. They stocked up on paper towels, paper napkins, and toilet paper.

With basket and cart bulging, they headed for the checkout counter. Ron reached into his back pocket, and then clutched Millie's arm so tightly his knuckles turned white. "My wallet. It's gone!" He set the basket on the floor and dashed up and down the aisles, certain he must have dropped it somewhere. That didn't make sense because he'd had no reason to take it out until he was ready to pay for the purchases, but that didn't slow him down.

Millie stepped aside and let the other customers take her place. Her heart pounded as she thought about what this would mean: calling the credit card companies, Ron getting a new driver's license, making a list of all the missing items—if they could even remember them. What a drag! Then Millie was mad—hopping mad. This forgetfulness was happening much too often these days. First a misplaced watch and then car keys and a prize coffee cup and now this—their cash and Ron's wallet.

"Dear God," she prayed, "what's up? Is there a message here we just aren't getting? Please send help ASAP. I'd rather not make a second trip."

Just then Millie remembered she had their checkbook in her purse. She'd put it there the day before to pay a neighbor for some carpentry work he'd done for them.

As Ron strode to the counter breathing hard and wringing his hands, Millie took him by the arm and whispered, "We'll be all right. I have the checkbook."

"But what about my wallet? My life is in it—every card that matters. What if someone gets hold of it?"

Millie ushered them through the checkout stand after writing the check and led her husband to the car. "Your life's in the Lord, not in your wallet," she reminded him. "Wait and see what God will do."

They drove home and Ron dashed into the house, ready to make the calls necessary to cancel their credit cards before someone could use them. As he reached for the phone, he noticed a familiar lump of bent brown leather on the kitchen sideboard—the "lost" wallet. "Hallelujah!" he exclaimed.

Then it dawned on him that he had taken it out just before they left to retrieve the haircut coupons. He'd forgotten to put it back into his pocket.

All was well. He hadn't lost his marbles—just his wallet, and that only temporarily. As he leafed through the billfold, he saw a scripture card he hadn't looked at in a long time: "We live by faith, not by sight" (2 Corinthians 5:7).

Reflection

Praise the Lord, O my soul, and forget not all
his benefits (Psalm 103:2).

———————

Lord, what a timely reminder, especially when I catch myself living by sight and not by faith. I make foolish mistakes that shake me up, but nothing rattles you. Thank you for doing for me what I can't do for myself.

Murder, He Said

❦

Drew loved watching movie reruns on TV or DVDs of old murder mysteries. He noted the titles in a notebook, and as he watched them he put the date and a check mark next to the title so he wouldn't watch or rent it again too soon. Now that he was 78 and counting, he noted that he'd watched a total of 453 films in the murder-mystery genre over the last four decades, give or take a few.

Dial M for Murder, Diagnosis Murder, and *Manhattan Murder Mystery* were among his favorites, but as he aged he wasn't as quick to recall the plot lines. He depended on the notebook to determine whether or not he'd seen a particular movie lately.

One Saturday afternoon Drew drove to Drive-Thru Flicks to pick up a few DVDs to pass the time while his wife, Eva, was away for the weekend babysitting their two granddaughters in a nearby town. He paced the aisles looking for a film he hadn't seen before. He scratched his head, wondering what to choose. Some titles *looked* familiar, but when he read the plot summaries on the back they didn't *sound* familiar. He felt like kicking himself for leaving his trusty notebook at home.

He chose a couple of flicks, paid for them, and drove off. *Wouldn't hurt to repeat one or two if that turned out to be the case,* he consoled himself. Later on Drew settled into his recliner in front of the new big-screen TV while balancing on his lap a bowl of popcorn drizzled with real butter and salt—something Eva would never have tolerated if she were home.

About an hour into the film the phone startled him. He hit the pause button on the remote and picked up the cordless receiver, which he'd placed on the side table next to his chair.

"Drew here," he said.

"Eva here," his wife teased.

Drew could hear the smile in her voice, and it warmed his heart. He missed her. But then he felt guilty when he looked at the empty popcorn bowl and the pot he hadn't yet cleaned and put away.

"Checking in," Eva reported. "The girls and I are calling to see how you're doing."

"Just fine," he said. "Munching popcorn and watching *Diagnosis Murder.* I'm about to find out 'who done it.'"

"But you've seen that movie at least a half dozen times. Remember when…"

"Don't tell me," he scolded. "I want to be surprised."

"How can you be surprised?" Eva sounded skeptical.

Drew bounced back with a chuckle in his voice. "I'm finding there's an advantage to memory fading with time. Even if I saw it before, it's a new movie every time 'cause I don't remember the plot."

Reflection

There is a time for everything, and a season for
every activity under heaven (Ecclesiastes 3:1).

————————

*Lord, there are some advantages to the golden years
after all!*

Eat Your Oats

❦

Roland volunteered at the Seascape Nursing Home. He felt it was the least he could do. The old folks needed a helping hand, and he was willing to lend one—or both. He enjoyed reading stories, serving meals, doing magic tricks, and playing the piano, anything to relieve the residents' boredom. He loved making life a bit brighter for these men and women who were more than 75 years old and confined to the facility for one reason or another.

Roland never counted himself as part of this group. He was 82, skinny as a tree branch, and straight as a stick. He walked five miles a day and was proud of it. His hair was thinning, and his muscle tone wasn't as sound as it used to be, but for a man his age he was a pretty fair specimen, if he did say so himself.

One Wednesday morning after breakfast in the common dining room, Roland walked in and played the piano for the oldsters. Afterward he took a seat in the audience and spent a while talking to the men and women.

Suddenly an elderly gentleman with a long beard and bent shoulders stood up and shouted to no one in particular, "Let's sing happy birthday to Roland. It's your birthday, ain't it?"

Roland stood and felt his face turn warm. "Not today. You must have me confused with someone else."

A woman with dyed red hair and pink polished fingernails pulled on Roland's shirtsleeve. "Don't be shy. You're old just like we are."

Roland was suddenly hot under the collar and wet under his arms. In fact he was more than hot and wet. He was mad and more than a little embarrassed. It was not his birthday, and even if it were, he wouldn't admit it here. Everyone in this place was really old. He was simply elderly.

Just then the recreation director walked in. "What's all this commotion about?" Mr. Peters asked. "Are you having fun or is someone in trouble?"

"Having fun," answered the bearded man.

The redhead poked Roland in the belly. "Making trouble," she squeaked. "It's his birthday. We want to sing, and he won't let us."

Mr. Peters wrinkled his brow. "Why not, Roland?"

"It's not my birthday, that's why!"

"I see. Well, apparently there's been some mistake. When is your birthday?"

"Next Tuesday."

"Well that's only a few days away. Suppose we sing now in case you're not with us that day."

Roland put up his hands in protest. He knew the routine, and he didn't like it one bit.

Mr. Peters sat down at the piano and plunked out the happy

birthday song. Those who could sing chimed in. Roland gritted his teeth through the song and managed a shallow "thank you" at the end. He sat down.

"How many candles on your cake this year?" asked Mr. Peters, as though he were speaking to a five year old.

"Too many," Roland replied.

"How old are you?" Mr. Peters seemed really curious now.

Roland exploded. He couldn't believe his own reaction. "None of your beeswax." He remembered his father saying that whenever someone asked him a question he didn't want to answer.

Mr. Peters remained implacable. He looked around the room. "Tell me your age, and I'll give you another bowl of oatmeal," he promised with a smile.

That did it. "Ask me again and I'll turn the bowl over on your head!"

Reflection

Pride goes before destruction, a haughty spirit before a fall (Proverbs 16:18).

———

Dear God, I know I can be shy—and sometimes testy—about revealing my age. I wonder why. What difference does a number make? All that matters is that I honor you with the years I have.

PART 3

TIME FLIES

Respect Your Elders

⟨⟨⟨⟨⟨⟨⟨⟨⟨

One afternoon Kitty and her mother, Virginia, decided to clean and polish Virginia's silverware in preparation for an estate sale before the elderly woman moved into an assisted-living facility. She was no longer able to live alone. Her forgetfulness was escalating and Kitty, who still worked full-time, was unable to take care of her mother around the clock.

Mother and daughter enjoyed sharing memories of the grandmothers and great-grandmothers who had passed on the treasures now being arranged for the sale. Virginia wanted to give some of the items to her daughters, but there were more than they could use, so a sale seemed the best way to go.

During the course of their conversation, Virginia picked up a set of hand-crocheted doilies, looked at them, and then tossed them on the floor. She was clearly agitated. She blinked and fidgeted with her hands and couldn't express a complete sentence without getting weepy.

Kitty probed a bit, and finally Virginia spilled her feelings about a family member who had given her the doilies as a gift, but then behind her back insulted her good name and had never apologized. She turned to Kitty. "Please don't laugh. This is serious."

"Mother, of course I won't laugh. I can tell this is very important to you. Tell me more."

But Virginia had moved on to something else. "I have a question for you. How old am I, and when was I born?"

"You're 83, Mom. You were born on May 2, 1924—a happy day for all of us who know and love you."

Virginia gasped. "I had no idea I was that old! Am I really 83?"

Kitty nodded and took her hand. "You are—and it's something to be proud of."

Virginia was not so easily placated. "Why couldn't you have just told me I was 25 or 31?" The women laughed but then Virginia grew somber again.

She repeated the name of the relative who had offended her. "How *dare* she speak about me that way! Why, I'm an old lady. Somebody needs to tell her to respect her elders."

Reflection

Remember the days of old; consider the
generations long past. Ask your father and he will
tell you, your elders, and they will explain to you
(Deuteronomy 32:7).

Dear God, please give me the grace to accept where I am and to be thankful for it.

Taking Turns

R obert put down the newspaper and caught the phone on the first ring. "Robert here."

"Howdy, Rob. It's Milton."

"Milton who?"

"Milton from Possum Trot."

"Hmmm."

"You don't remember me, do you?"

"Can't say I do. I haven't lived there for years. What's our connection?"

"Your bicycle."

"I don't own a bike. Haven't had one of my own since I was ten years old."

"I know. That's the one I'm talking about."

Robert was about to hang up. This man wasn't making sense.

"I looked you up in the Los Angeles phone directory on the Internet. Got me a computer this year. My kids hooked me up to the twenty-first century."

"And?" Robert's pulse elevated. He was irritated.

"I just wanted to check in after all these years. We went to grade school together. Remember Miss Bertie Mae? She taught us in fourth grade—the year you got your Schwinn bicycle with the shiny handlebars."

Robert scratched his head. He barely remembered the bike his father had worked so hard to get him. And here was a stranger who recalled the manufacturer and the color.

"I s'pose you're wonderin' why I called."

"As a matter of fact I am."

"To thank you for letting me ride your bike. I was thinking about it the other day and thought that was a darned nice thing you did for me. I never had a bike, but I felt like I did because you shared yours with me. It means a lot, even after all these years."

Robert felt tears well up in his eyes.

"Well, that's what I called about. I'll let you go now. Nice talkin' to you. And if you ever come back to Possum Trot, drop on by."

In an instant Milton was gone. He didn't even leave his phone number so Robert could call back.

Robert smiled to himself. *Guess I can look you up on the Internet. As you said, Milton, this is the twenty-first century. We can rekindle our friendship—and maybe even plan a bike ride!*

Reflection

Let us not love with words or tongue but with
actions and in truth (1 John 3:18).

———————

Lord, how little I know about how my actions influence and inspire others. Help me share something of myself today that will brighten someone else's day, even if it's just a smile, a nod, a word, or a phone call.

A Funny Thing Happened on My Way to Pray

⸎

Ellie set out her devotional, Bible, journal, and pen. She slipped into her pink chenille bathrobe and matching slippers and padded into the living room. She turned on the lamp over the rocker next to the window overlooking the garden. All set.

Not quite. She forgot her cup of tea sitting on the counter in the kitchen. *I must have my tea. Prayer time simply isn't the same without it,* she reminded herself. But as she passed the fridge, Ellie saw a note she had posted there the night before: Take Ralph's blue suit to the cleaners.

Good thing I wrote that reminder or the suit would have stayed in the closet all week. When it came time to put it on for Iris and John's anniversary dinner and dance, Ralph would have been so disappointed. The soup spatter from last week would still be there.

Ellie went to the closet right away, took out the suit, and put it by the front door.

Now where was I? On my way to pray, that's right.

The tea. She picked up the cup but noticed it had cooled off so she popped it into the microwave for a quick nuke. A moment later it was piping hot again. Ellie dropped in a dollop of honey, and then walked back to the living room. As she sat down, she saw a spider spinning a dainty little web in the corner above the piano. *Drat! I hate to disturb his endeavor, but I simply can't bear spiders sharing my home.*

Ellie grabbed a tissue from her pocket, lifted the poor fellow out of the web, and let him loose in the garden. *I hope he'll find a lovely spot among the flowers to rebuild his home. There are so many pretty places to choose from.*

Back to the living room and her favorite chair. Finally it was time to curl up, talk to God, and make a few notations in her journal. There was so much to thank Him for. Ellie enjoyed creating her own hymn of praise, singing to the Lord with pen and paper, musing about the wonderful things He had done in her life. The gift of her dear husband, Ralph, was on top of Ellie's list. Mindy, her cat, was right up there too. And, of course, her three adult children and all the grandkids.

"I picked up my pen, opened the journal, and was jarred out of my senses with the sound of the phone. Wouldn't you know it? I had forgotten to bring it with me. I was so busy with tea and prayer books and itsy bitsy spider!"

It was Ellie's neighbor Barbara calling. She needed a ride to the hairdresser. With a broken right arm, she couldn't drive for at least six weeks. Ellie agreed to help, of course, but Barbara wanted to leave in 30 minutes.

"Here I was hardly dressed to go out, and I still hadn't started my prayer time." Ellie was frustrated with all the distractions, but then a funny thing happened. The Lord dropped into her mind the verse that says to pray without ceasing.

Perfect timing, she thought. *It's nice when I can settle down in one place and focus on a list of things to write about and read and pray for in a logical and orderly way. But it's also perfectly fine to pray moment-by-moment while I pour a cup of tea, make the bed, take Ralph's suit to the cleaners, and visit with Barbara while we drive to her appointment.*

Ellie thought about how God is everywhere and ever with her, in the mundane and in the mysteries of life. Prayer time is any time and all the time. *My very life can be a prayer. God is pleased with me just the way I am, wherever I am. I love Him, and I know He loves me!*

Reflection

Pray without ceasing (1 Thessalonians 5:17 KJV).

———————

God, it is so easy to become distracted by the cares of the world, the small duties that so easily consume my day, and the people who flow in and out of my life. Help me to include all of this in my daily prayers as I walk with you from sunrise to sunset.

Condolences

Margaret hated revealing her age. It was a private affair as far as she was concerned—like politics and religion and hair color. No one's business but hers, and that was final. So when her daughter and son-in-law threw her a surprise party for her seventieth, she was more ruffled than grateful.

The array of cards and gifts softened her a bit, and the chance to be photographed with her many friends and family members appealed to her. Wouldn't it be nice to have a beautiful keepsake album to look at when she was *really* old?

After all the well-wishers had left, gifts reopened, and cards displayed for a second look, Margaret noticed that she'd missed one. It had come in the mail that day and apparently fell to the side amid the pile of gifts.

She tore it open, eager to see what her 80-year-old sister in Florida had to say. "What is this?" Margaret wondered aloud. "It's a sympathy card." She was certain Millicent had lost her marbles. *Condolences—for what?* she wondered.

Margaret opened the card and laughed out loud. Millicent was perfectly sound and sane. This card was just one more of her goofy pranks. "My heartfelt sympathy," it read, "on the loss of your *youth*. May you take comfort in the fact that you don't look a day over 75!"

"Why that little rascal!" Margaret rocked with laughter and then reached for the phone. It was her turn to reverse the process. She'd call her sister and remind her that if she (Margaret) didn't look a day over 75, Millicent didn't look a day over 85!

Reflection

I will sing to the LORD all my life; I will sing
praise to my God as long as I live
(Psalm 104:33).

———————

Lord, am I too conscious of my age, embarrassed to admit that I really am growing older? What is there to be ashamed of? As long as I believe in you and walk with you every day, I am a new creature and my chronological age is of no consequence.

Lookin' Good

⸎⸎⸎

Grandma Elsa, Phyllis' grandmother, always fibbed about her age. She got away with it because she looked younger than her years. Her husband died when Grandma was 53. To look at her then, she appeared about 40. But her fibbing created a real problem in the family. It made it difficult for Phyllis' mother and aunts to tell their true age because Grandma would have been taken for a child bride!

According to Phyllis, "The saga of 'Grandma's age' went on through the month she was eligible for Social Security. Grandma timed it so she was the last one in the Social Security office on the day she was to fill out her application. Instead of stating her age aloud, she wrote it on a piece of paper and handed it face down to the clerk. He flashed her a knowing smile as if to say, 'This will be *our* little secret.'"

But there came a time when Elsa's game backfired. At age 80 she met a gentleman of 63, who assumed by her looks that she was around 60. She did nothing to dissuade him of this thought!

The two dated for several months and soon everyone in her family was sure Clem would pop the question any time. Then one evening, while standing in line for a movie, Elsa's purse fell off her arm and the contents spilled on the ground.

Clem bent down to scoop up her lipstick, comb, breath mints, and wallet. There was her driver's license in the front plastic pocket of her billfold. Clem remarked on the photo, and then looked stricken. There was no mistaking her age from the birthdate printed in plain view.

That did it. Clem took Elsa home that evening, and she never heard from him again. "I guess a 17-year difference on Grandma's end was just too much for the 60-plus youngster," said Phyllis, chuckling at the picture in her mind.

Her grandmother died four years later, and even then Phyllis said her mother couldn't bear to end the fibbing. She shaved off ten years when she sent the obituary to the local newspaper. The editor, herself getting up in years, understood and went right along with it.

"To me Grandma Elsa will always be ageless," Phyllis stated. "She was just that kind of person—forever young in heart."

Reflection

Is not wisdom found among the aged? Does not long life bring understanding? (Job 12:12).

Lord, I like to joke about my age, even to fib a bit for the fun of it. But the years we are on earth are nothing to you, for you are above and beyond the bounds of time. You love us with an everlasting love. You have promised us an eternity of days with you when we pass from this earth.

Musical Hit Parade

Monique was invited to present a program of piano music at a retirement home. She selected popular songs of the 1930s and 1940s, some favorite hymns, and patriotic numbers that residents could relate to.

"While playing hymns," said Monique, "I had a strange feeling someone was standing behind me. I glanced back to see a frail, silver-haired man glancing over my shoulder, much like my father used to do when I played and sang his favorite songs at home."

Monique nodded and smiled, encouraging the elderly gentleman to join in. He smiled back and started singing along in a soft, tremulous voice. He knew every word of the venerable hymn. "His eye is on the sparrow, and I know He watches me," we sang.

"The audience sat in rapt silence as he asked me to play more and more of his favorites. There was no question that he was having a wonderful time singing the hymns of his youth."

He was not the only one having a good time. Monique's eyes

glistened as she played and recalled the happy memories of her childhood. "It was pure serendipity for me," she added. "I felt as if I were at home again, hearing Daddy singing his special songs while I played the piano for him."

Soon Monique, the man beside her, and the entire roomful of white and silver-haired men and women, some in wheelchairs, others seated at tables, some hobbling across the room with the help of a walker or cane, joined in until the retirement home rocked with the sounds of praise and thanksgiving to the God they loved and served.

Reflection

Sing joyfully to the LORD, you righteous;
    it is fitting for the upright to praise him.
Praise the LORD with the harp;
    make music to him on the ten-stringed lyre.
Sing to him a new song;
    play skillfully, and shout for joy (Psalm 33:1-4).

———————————

Dear Lord, you love it when we praise you with singing and dancing and the sound of instruments glorifying your holy name. Whether we are young and robust, or elderly and frail, we can lift you up and honor your presence with songs of joy and gratitude.

PART 4

SWEET
SOMETHINGS

Hot Dog!

❧⤳⤶❧

H omer loves hot dogs and has ever since he was a kid when his grandpa took him to the ballpark. Dogs and chips and soda were as important to the baseball experience as the final score. But Homer is 67 now, and the trim physique of his youth has given way to a bit of a front porch. Paula, his wife, is very conscious of it. In fact, she admits she spends too much time reminding Homer that he needs to knock off the hot dogs and learn to love seafood and veggies. He waves her off, avoiding her nutritional advice. He figures he got this far in life eating his way, so why change now.

One Saturday afternoon Paula had a yen for the specialty at Logan's Deli on Main Street. "Homer, would you run out to Logan's and pick up a couple of Greek wraps? We could have a little picnic in the backyard like old times. I'll fix some lemonade and whip up a batch of the vanilla wafers you like so much."

Homer pulled on his chin and furrowed his brow. "I'm in favor of the picnic and the cookies, but a Greek wrap? No way. My idea

of a wrap is a soft little bun around a juicy hot hog. I'll get a wrap
for you and a dog for me. How's that?"

"No way!" Paula put her hands on her hips. "You know how I
feel about fatty hot dogs."

Homer put his hands on his hips. "And you know how *I* feel
about them." He noticed the frustration in his wife's eyes. He
decided to make a deal. "Tell you what. If I find a parking place
in front of Logan's, I get to have a hot dog. If I have to park down
the block, I'll go along with you and get a wrap."

Paula let out a deep breath and laughed. "You're on! There
hasn't been a free space in front of Logan's on a Saturday for two
decades. Can't imagine there being one today, but hey, if there is,
you deserve to win."

Homer took off whistling. He just knew today was the day
he'd have his hard-won hot dog. He pulled onto Main Street a little later, parked, walked into Logan's, ordered the wrap and hot
dog, paid for them, and sailed home, feeling pretty good about
himself. He'd won—and he had done so honestly. He'd parked in
front, just as he bargained for.

He walked into the kitchen. Paula was waiting, lemonade
ready, cookies cooling on the counter.

"Well?" she queried.

Homer noticed the self-satisfied glint in her eye. "Well what?
Here's your wrap and here's my dog."

Paula's blue eyes deepened. "You found a parking place in front
of Logan's on a Saturday? Amazing! How'd you do that?"

Homer sank into his chair, stifling a laugh. He held onto his
hot dog with a death grip. "I had to drive around the block six
times first, but I did get one."

Reflection

Truthful lips endure forever, but a lying tongue
lasts only a moment (Proverbs 12:19).

———————

Lord, I admit it. I'm stubborn and shortsighted some-times. I know what you're teaching me, but I resist because I want my own way, whether eating a hot dog, watching a TV show I should avoid, or winning an argument. Please help me to stop making deals and willingly submit to your voice.

Face-lift

Ruth looked in the mirror. She didn't like what she saw. She tugged at the chin folds, pulled the skin around her eyes, and held in her belly. There wasn't much she could do about the stretch marks there or the veins that were now prominent in her hands.

I wonder if a face-lift would help me feel better about myself? But I wouldn't be fooling anyone except strangers. All my friends and family know what I look like. How terrible it would be if they didn't recognize me.

Still, it was fun to push and probe and prod her face, trying out new looks. She *could* appear younger, no question about it. But cosmetic surgery was so expensive. Ruth stepped back from the mirror, took off her glasses, and realized she didn't look half bad when she stopped examining herself so closely.

That night over dinner Ruth told her husband about her daydream of recapturing her youthful appearance, becoming the "girl" he'd fallen in love with some 40 years before. "What do you say?" she teased. "Are you willing to spring for a few grand so I can lop off a dozen or so years?"

Frank's eyebrows shot together like two furry caterpillars in a fight. "Not on your life! I like the *woman* I'm married to. The girl you were was great then, but this is now and I love you as you are."

"Wrinkles and bunions and bulges and all?"

"And blue eyes and a killer smile and warm hands and a tender heart."

Ruth sank into her husband's lap and laced her arms around his neck. "Oh, Frank! You're so romantic."

He looked up and winked. "Besides, if you got a face-lift, what would people think? That you were living with your father?"

Reflection

Charm is deceptive, and beauty is fleeting; but
a woman who fears the LORD is to be praised
(Proverbs 31:30).

Lord, it's tempting to think of ways to recover my youthful looks—even if some of them are extreme and expensive. The world tantalizes me with its wares and promises. But you remind me that real beauty is deeper than skin. A person of beauty is someone who walks with you all the days of his or her life. And that's exactly what I want to do.

No Wooden Nickels

❧⟨☙

G racie and Harold planned to celebrate their fiftieth wedding anniversary with dinner and dessert at Chez Andre—their favorite restaurant. June 8 was the one day of the year when Harold would spring for a truly special evening. Most of the time he guarded his pennies, nickels, quarters, and dollars like a shepherd guarding a flock of sheep.

"I had to make a strong case every time I suggested a purchase or a vacation or a meal out," Gracie groused.

"I'll think about it," was Harold's standard reply to nearly every request for money.

After more years of this than Gracie could stand, she decided to take matters into her own hands. Whenever Harold stalled with "I'll think about it," Gracie responded, "I'll give you ten minutes, and if I don't hear back by then, I'll assume the answer is yes."

Harold would laugh and look at his watch. "You're on." He welcomed the challenge. However, he usually overlooked the fact that he was getting a bit forgetful in his old age. Two minutes, ten minutes, an hour. They were all about the same to him. Gracie, on the other hand, counted on her husband's forgetfulness. It worked in her favor when she wanted a few bucks for an important purchase.

The one she had in mind for their anniversary was really important. She approached Harold the morning of June 8. "Honey, can you trust me with a few dollars?"

Harold looked over his coffee cup and muttered, "I'll think about it."

She gave her standard reply. Then Gracie glanced at the kitchen clock: *Ten minutes till yes.*

She cleaned up the breakfast dishes and when the clock read 10:07 she grabbed the checkbook out of the desk drawer and headed for the car. An hour later she returned, giddy with the purchase she'd hidden in the garage.

Harold whirled around in his easy chair. "Where've you been? I must have dozed off."

"Shopping."

"But I'm still thinking about it," Harold complained.

"Your ten minutes was up an hour ago," Gracie said in a sweet voice.

"This better be a good one." Harold pushed himself out of the chair. "Okay, how much did I lose?"

"You lost an old workbench."

Harold hustled out to the garage. There stood a new compact workbench with a matching stool—something he'd always wanted but was too cheap to buy for himself.

Tears welled in his eyes. He turned to Gracie and put his arms around her. "You got me this time," he said and kissed her like he hadn't done for a long time.

"Oh, Harold!" she said. "I just love it when you think about it!"

Reflection

Listen carefully to my words; let your ears take
in what I say (Job 13:17).

———————————

Lord, when you ask me to do something for my own good, how often I mutter, "I'll think about it." It's embarrassing to admit, but it's true. Today I want to change that behavior. Instead of thinking about what you said, help me simply do it.

Due Credit

⏤⚬⚮⚬⏤

Sid had five dollars worth of credit at Hannah's House and Garden. It burned a hole in his pocket. He couldn't wait to return to the store and put it toward some new gizmo for his workshop.

He got to the store and walked up and down the aisles. *A new saw? Maybe. Oh, that weather-stripping looks good. Hey, what about a new set of lights for the front walkway?*

There were too many choices. He rounded the corner into the aisle with garden accessories and there it was—the perfect item. He was so glad he'd come in this morning. A fancy birdbath. He could apply his credit, and that would make it a great deal. *Irene will love this. She's always wanted to attract more birds to our yard.*

Sid lugged the box onto a shopping cart and wheeled it to the checkstand. He pulled out the credit slip and his credit card to take care of the balance. He walked out to his truck, loaded the cargo into the back, and headed home.

He pulled into the garage, and his wife called hello from the side yard where she was weeding and watering the flowerbed. Sid could hardly wait to surprise her. He unpacked the birdbath and scooted it along the walkway. "Surprise!" he shouted.

Irene squealed at the sight of the cute fixture. She took off her sun hat, mopped her forehead, and wrapped her arm around Sid's neck. "Thank you! I love it, and I know the birds will too."

Sid positioned it near their dogwood tree, filled the bowl with water, and stepped back to admire it.

Irene smiled at Sid. She was obviously pleased with the surprise. "By the way, how much did it cost?"

Sid cocked his head and smiled broadly. "It was a steal!"

"Really? On sale?" Irene seemed doubtful that such a beautiful item could be "a steal."

"One hundred dollars out the door," he said, "but I had a credit slip. So we saved."

"How much credit?" She looked wary now.

"Five dollars," Sid boasted.

Irene sank into a nearby lawn chair. "You spent $100 in order to save $5?"

"Don't I get a little credit?" he asked.

"Sorry, Sid," Irene comforted. "I think the store gets the credit for this one!"

Just then a blue jay landed on the edge of the new birdbath, hopped into the water, and fluttered its wings.

Irene turned to Sid.

"I take that back. The bird and I are willing to give credit where credit is due. Thank you for this delightful surprise."

Reflection

Look at the birds of the air; they do not sow or
reap or store away in barns, and yet your
heavenly Father feeds them (Matthew 6:26).

———————

*Lord, thank you for surprises and delights, for needs
and wants. You deserve all my praise and thanksgiving—and all the credit!*

Nuts and Bolts

One Saturday morning in April, Donna and Ray looked at each other over breakfast with a knowing grin. This was the day they had set aside to tackle a job they'd been putting off for months—simplifying their lives. From clearing calendars to cleaning closets, it was a daunting task but they agreed there was no turning back.

"When we're finished, I'll take you to dinner at Café Pinot," Ray promised.

"You're on," Donna replied. She could already taste the Chocolate Hazelnut Galette, one of the chef's specialties. She pulled on her jeans and a sweatshirt and set to work. Donna started on the closet in the hall, pulling out unused clothing, books, and household goods. In their home/office, Ray plowed through boxes of old files and yellowing paper. By mid-morning they were cookin'.

"This is fun!" Donna shouted across the hallway. "It feels so good to toss this junk. I might not buy another thing for the rest of my life!"

"Promise?" Ray teased as he popped his head around the corner.

The more they tossed, the lighter they felt. By late afternoon Donna was suddenly aware that simplifying her physical house was just the beginning. Her emotional and spiritual house needed a good spring cleaning as well.

"The closets in my soul were filled with clutter too—relationships I no longer enjoyed, household routines that wore me out, self-defeating thoughts that stifled my creativity." While on her knees pulling boxes and bags from under the bed, Donna decided to stop and pray. What had begun as a day of simple housecleaning was turning into a day of spiritual transformation. "Lord, I've been out of control," she moaned. "Take over, please. Help me simplify my life so there will be room for what really matters—time with family, time to walk with you, time to play."

Donna carried on, poking through old books on a high shelf, bringing order to a box of camping equipment, filing tax papers in colored folders. By the end of the day, she'd filled six large trash bags with items they no longer needed or wanted.

"Not only were our closets clutter-free, so were my mind and heart," she said.

That evening as Donna and Ray enjoyed coffee and chocolate at Café Pinot, Donna told Ray she believed God was leading them into a new season of simplicity, free of striving and acquiring. A knowing smile crossed his face.

"Then and there we committed to ask God to be part of every activity, decision, and purchase," Donna said, "whether a new piece of furniture or a new friendship."

Reflection

Now that you have been set free from sin...the
benefit you reap leads to holiness, and the result
is eternal life (Romans 6:22).

———————————

*Dear Lord, by simplifying my time and space, I am
more able to walk with you in humility and grace.*

Beautician or Magician?

ana and Lou walked through their hair salon one last time. Lana began weeping. They had owned the place for 50 years and had served a clientele that spanned the county. In recent years they had added a service for seniors with special needs, including washing and styling and manicures in a separate room suited to people who needed a wheelchair or walker. That brought even more customers into their attractive shop on the west side of town. But now they were not only seniors themselves, but *elderly* seniors and running a business had become too much. It was time to sell the shop, retire, and relax.

They didn't worry about their own beauty needs because they could still do each other's hair. In fact Lana had depended on Lou for such help throughout their marriage.

Lana pulled a photo album from the shelf above her station and began paging through it, pointing to one hairstyle after another and chuckling when she saw the many changes that had occurred in the last five decades.

Lou joined her and had a few laughs himself. "Those were some get-ups," he said. "And we went right along with it. Amazing."

Curly perms, bangs and bobs, hippy hair-dos, and butch cuts. The book included a wide range of styles that had come and gone.

Lou reached for the coffee cup on the table at his station. He read the wording and burst out laughing: I'M A BEAUTICIAN, NOT A MAGICIAN.

"Do you remember who gave it to you?" Lana asked.

Lou scratched his head and frowned. "Vaguely. Can't pull her name, right off."

"Marybelle Simpson," said Lana. "You got so upset with her one day that you let it out. 'What do you think I am, a magician?' you asked. Marybelle couldn't be happy no matter what you did." Lana paused for a moment and smiled. "For Christmas that year she gave you this cup. She was so excited about it. It was one of those items a person just happens on. You both had a good laugh."

"Never did like the beauty business," Lou mumbled.

"What did you say?" Lana's eyes revealed her surprise.

Lou raised his voice. "I never liked doing hair—never."

Lana was shocked. "What are you saying? *Now* you tell me—after all these years? What did you want to do? And why didn't you speak up?"

"I wanted to paint—you know, watercolors—but I figured I couldn't support a family on it."

"I'm upset thinking you were unhappy all these years, and you never owned up to it. What a waste." Lana's heart sagged.

"Oh it wasn't a waste, dear," said Lou with a twinkle in his eye. "I got to spend every day with *you*."

Reflection

Let beauty treatments be given to them
(Esther 2:3).

———————

Dear God, we don't always get what we want in life, but what does it matter as long as we have you. Spending time in your presence is all that counts.

Candy Hearts

Nancy's husband, Jerry, knows her weakness for sweets. Every couple of weeks or so he brings home a box of caramel corn or toffee-covered pecans or a lemon meringue pie.

On Valentine's Day this year, Nancy awoke and stumbled into her office, sleep still in her eyes. She flipped on the computer and there next to her mouse was a small dish with several candy hearts, each with an encouraging phrase imprinted on it.

How thoughtful! she remarked to herself. "I popped a couple into my mouth, padded to the kitchen, plugged in the coffeemaker, and pulled out the frying pan," she said. "There on the counter were a few more hearts, so I shoved those into my mouth as well."

Nancy walked back to the bedroom, patted her face with a warm wet washcloth, and ran a brush through her tangled hair. "I leaned toward the mirror and on the shelf below it were three more candy hearts. *What the heck!* I thought. *It's Valentine's Day. Candy before breakfast is all right on such a special occasion.*"

Jerry came up behind Nancy and slid his arms around her waist. "Happy Valentine's Day," he chirped. "Did you like my surprise?"

"I love it. Thank you so much. You always knock me out when I least expect it. When did you plant all these hearts?"

"After you fell asleep," he said and kissed her on the neck. "How about some breakfast?"

"Meet you in the kitchen!"

Nancy cracked three eggs on the side of the skillet and dropped them into the melting butter. She opened the trash can to toss the eggshells and noticed a bunch of candy hearts.

"Jerry, what's this?" she asked, pointing to the discarded candies in the trash container. "Broken hearts?" she teased, pleased with her early morning banter.

"No. I tossed those, my love," he said, snuggling up to her in that romantic way of his, "because they didn't say what I wanted to express to you."

Nancy gulped, took her glasses out of the pocket of her bathrobe, and quickly put them on. She looked at Jerry, feeling a bit sheepish. "You mean I was supposed to *read* the candy hearts before I ate them?"

As Nancy recalled later, "So much for romance that day! I dished up the eggs then slid under the table in shame! Jerry joined me, and we had a good laugh and a Valentine's Day hug."

Reflection

Your love is more delightful than wine
(Song of Solomon 1:2).

_____

Lord, I complain when I don't get enough attention from my spouse, and then I forget to acknowledge it when I do. My mate is a good person. I want to focus on the fruit, not the faults, in his/her life. Help me be encouraging so that our love will be sweet.

Costly Secret

❦

Sid woke up on Monday morning, walked to the park and back, ate breakfast, and enjoyed a cup of coffee with his wife, Dede, on the patio overlooking their rose garden. He excused himself to go to the bathroom. After taking care of business, he turned, glanced in the toilet bowl and panicked. He saw blood. His first thought was to rush out and tell Dede, but he didn't want to upset her. "I'll handle this myself," he said to his reflection in the mirror.

Over the next several weeks Sid made several medical appointments, first with his primary care provider and then with a gastroenterologist. He went through the discomfort of an Upper GI, Lower GI, barium enema, and finally a colonoscopy at the hospital. When he had to follow a special diet—for the tests—he told Dede he just wasn't feeling well. And each time he left the house, he told Dede he was running an errand, picking up gardening supplies, meeting a friend for coffee, or spending the day golfing. She didn't ask any questions since these were routine outings for Sid over the course of their marriage.

Meanwhile, Sid was sleeping fitfully, his heart was palpitating at just the thought of the next procedure, and he lost his appetite. His mind had a field day. He imagined surgery at the very least and colon cancer at the worst.

On several occasions he came close to telling Dede, but then backed down. He missed sharing such a serious milestone in his life, and he longed for the comfort of her arms and her prayers. But still he couldn't bring himself to talk about it until he had more information to share. He didn't want to scare her.

A week after the final procedure he received word from his doctor that all test results were negative. He was given a clean bill of health. The lab work did not show any sign of blood. What a relief! *Maybe it was simply a hemorrhoid,* Sid thought. *Why didn't I think of that sooner?*

Sid was so elated that he went to Dede immediately. "Put on your prettiest dress," he said. "I'm taking you out for dinner tonight—maybe even dancing, if you can keep up with me!" He felt as though he could take on the world.

"What's gotten into you?" she asked, wrinkling her brow in confusion. "You hate to dance, and you're not all that excited about eating out. You don't like spending money on food we can cook at home."

"I have something important to tell you. I want to do so over a candlelight dinner."

"All right," she agreed. "I'll be ready."

That night the couple walked into Harbor Lights Restaurant and were led to a cozy booth overlooking the water.

"I can't wait another minute," said Dede. "What is it? Did you win the lottery? Book a cruise? Buy a new car? Tell me, please."

Sid smiled, reached across the table and took her hand. Then he gave her a detailed report on what had been going on secretly over the last couple of months. "So now you know," he said and squeezed her hand. "Looks like you're stuck with me for a few more years. I hope you're as happy about it as I am."

Dede returned his gaze and then threw her head back in a hearty laugh. "Oh Sid! You are precious! Remember when Nan and Paul gave us fresh beets from their garden about two months ago? Well…"

"What's that got to do with my good news?" Sid probed, feeling hurt by her laughter.

"Beet juice is about the same color as blood. It runs right through us. I can see where you'd mistake the color of the beets for blood in your stool."

Sid sank in his seat and sighed. Then he sat up and laughed. "What a chump!" he said. "All that time and money and embarrassment. A costly secret. If I had told you the first day, I could have saved myself a lot of worry and trouble."

"But if you *had* told me," said Dede, "we wouldn't be sitting here having a romantic, candlelight dinner. And dancing after dessert!"

Sid reached over and kissed Dede in front of he didn't care who. "You're the best!" he exclaimed.

Reflection

"Can anyone hide in secret places so that I cannot see him?" declares the Lord (Jeremiah 23:24).

———————————

Lord, you know my innermost secrets and desires, fears, and trepidations. May I look to you first when I am afraid, instead of taking matters into my own hands and then being disappointed with the results.

Time's Up

Chaz and his wife, Arlette, prepared for a crew to come in and begin updating their kitchen. That meant emptying shelves, cabinets, cubbyholes, and the pantry—no small chore after living in their house for 35 years.

A week before the start date, Arlette was called out of town on business. This left the dirty work to Chaz.

"Before you leave," he said, "I'd like us to agree on something so I don't have to phone you about whether to keep or toss every little item."

"Fine. How do you want to work it?"

"Let's agree that if we haven't used an item in two years or more, I pitch it or give it to a charity."

Arlette looked up, touched her chin in thought, opened and closed drawers and cabinets, then gave Chaz a nod of approval. "You're on," she said. "I don't think there will be much to debate, but I'm happy to go along with your plan."

She left the next morning. Chaz rolled up his shirt sleeves that day and started sorting and assessing everything from an old pot without a lid to a pair of rusty tongs. He made three piles: Keep, Toss, Give Away.

By noon he was feeling great. He had reduced the clutter to the point that everything left fit nicely on the dining room table and on the floor beneath it.

The workers arrived two days later, and the demolition process began.

The following week, Arlette came home and was delighted to find that Chaz had not gone overboard, as she suspected he might. He was the tosser in the family, and she was the keeper.

Eight weeks later the kitchen was ready for use. Chaz and Arlette awakened the next day ready to return every item to its new and rightful place. But as Arlette went through the baking pans, cooking pots, and mixing bowls, some of her favorite cooking tools were missing.

"Chaz, where did you put…? What did you do with…? I can't find…"

"Sorry, hon," he said with a grin. "Time was up on all that stuff. Haven't used them in two years or more, remember?"

"This is horrible," she said, "I never should have agreed to such a deal. Wouldn't you know it? *Tonight* is the very night I planned to make a pot roast in our Dutch oven, bake muffins in our cupcake tin, and whip potatoes with the old hand blender!"

"Sure!" he teased. "You haven't made a meal like that in the last five years."

Arlette folded her arms and lifted her head. "Well then, you'll just have to take me out to dinner—every night this week—because the menu I had planned requires nearly every item you gave away. Too bad I wasn't home to advise you of my plans!"

Chaz caught the twinkle in her eye. He wrapped his arms around Arlette and drew her close. "I'll let you get away with it this week," he said, "but starting Monday night, we'll be using all the *new* cookware I purchased while you were away." Then he pulled out a large box from the hall closet and presented it to her with a big kiss.

Reflection

A generous man will himself be blessed
(Proverbs 22:9).

———————

Dear Lord, it's fun to laugh and share and tease the people I love. I sense that you are delighted when we do loving things for one another. You are the model of generosity. Thank you for showing me how to give from my abundance, which came from you.

Night Out

⤜⊙⤚

Gary approached his wife, Joann, as she settled into her recliner in the den. "Want to do something tonight?"

"Like what?"

"I don't know. Maybe a movie, or a drive around the lake, or even dancing at the Mayfair Lounge."

"Sorry to be a party-pooper," Joann said, "but I'd rather stay home. I don't feel like getting dressed and fighting traffic."

Gary shrugged, grabbed the remote, and turned on the History channel. "Maybe something here will hold our interest," he said and settled into his easy chair.

Joann offered to make a pitcher of lemonade and pop some corn.

"Not *another* program on World War II!" Gary exclaimed. He surfed the channels and then suddenly stood up and pulled Joann by the hand.

"This is pathetic! Let's *do* something. If you don't want to see a movie or go dancing, how about walking through Barnes & Noble? We can browse the travel books, get a cup of mocha in their cafe, and read a few magazines. Beats falling asleep in front of the tube like an old couple!"

Joann agreed as long as she could wear what she had on—jeans and a T-shirt.

"You look fine," said Gary. "It's just a bookstore, not a resort."

The two drove to the mall and walked into the store. They agreed to split up for a few minutes, each visiting a favorite aisle, and then meet in the travel section. Gary combed the gardening books while Joann looked at the self-help titles.

Twenty minutes later they picked out a couple of travel books to study, and Joann plopped down in one of the comfy chairs near the cafe. Gary ordered two mochas. When he returned to Joann, she was nodding off. He sat down next to her and realized he couldn't shake his own sleepiness.

"So much for a night on the town," he muttered, laughing to himself. He stood up, tapped his wife on the shoulder, and said, "Let's go. We can do *this* at home."

They pulled into their garage a few minutes later, padded into the den, sank into their recliners, and broke out laughing. There they were—back where they had started from.

Gary flipped on the History channel willing to give it one more chance.

"I think I'll make some popcorn," Joann quipped, then put her head back. Within minutes Gary heard her snoring softly.

Reflection

Now may the Lord of peace himself give you
peace at all times and in every way
(2 Thessalonians 3:16).

Dear Lord, I thank you that I can rest in peace in my home with the spouse you gave me. How good it is to take it easy after a long day and to be content with what I have and with who I am.

In Darkness and in Light

Norm and Angie dated for three years before they were married. That is, if you call dating getting together for coffee or a movie or a walk when they could spare a couple of hours. Between them they had six kids—ages 14 to 20! There was always something going on with his brood or hers—soccer games, piano lessons, Girl Scouts, Little League, and so on. Sometimes the only chance Norm and Angie had to visit was over the phone while Angie stirred spaghetti sauce with one hand and held the phone with the other. Norm often called from his car while he drove to a client's office. Angie called him on her break at work.

Finally she'd had enough of this part-time romance. Angie's 14-year-old must have read her mind.

"When are we getting married?" Julia asked as Angie drove her to school one April morning.

"*We?*" Angie probed. "Aren't you and whomever you have in mind a little young to be thinking about matrimony?"

"Not *me,* Mom!" she spouted. "I mean you and Norm and all us kids?"

"Oh, *that* we! Do you think it's a good idea?"

"Yes…and so do Jamie and Lonnie and Patricia and Sam and Lily."

"It sounds as if you've taken a vote. Do Norm and I have anything to say about this?"

"You could say *yes!*"

Angie and Julia laughed, hugged goodbye, and blew each other a kiss. "See you at three, honey," Angie called.

"See ya, Mom."

Angie drove off, mulling what her daughter had said. Moments later she pulled over to the side of the road and reached for her cell phone. *Julia's right. It's time to make this happen.* Angie decided then and there to call Norm before she lost her courage.

"Hi, sweets. It's Angie. I have a proposal for you."

"Let's have it." Norm sounded rushed. *Maybe he has a client in the car. I should have asked.*

"Will you marry me?" she squeaked.

Norm gulped. "You serious?"

"Dead serious. We're both over 50. Time's running out. We need to be together. What do you say? Our kids are all for it. Julia told me."

"I say *yes!* I thought you'd never ask!" he responded.

"*I'd* never ask?" Then Angie gulped. "Great. When?"

"How about the last week in June, right after Lily graduates?"

"Sounds perfect! Gotta run. I have a wedding to plan."

Over the next month Angie felt like a monkey in a tree. She swung between a formal wedding at her church to a family thing at home. Finally they settled on a small evening ceremony at a chapel in Fairfield, a little town about 30 minutes from home. An evening wedding sounded romantic.

Friends and family pitched in to arrange flowers, food, and invitations.

The day of the wedding, Angie woke up scared. All preparations were finished. Suddenly she was filled with questions and doubts. *Am I ready? Is this what I really want?*

Heck of a time to recoil! her mind shot back.

God, help me, please. Was this your idea or mine? I can't remember. Getting married is a big step. Taking on three more kids, sharing a bathroom with someone after all these years. Norm said he snores, and he doesn't eat lasagna. That's my favorite dish. I think we're incompatible, don't you?

Of course I love him, but is that enough, Lord? Just a week ago I was so happy. Will you promise to pick me up if I keel over?

At five thirty, Julia, Patricia, Sam, and Angie piled into the car and drove to the chapel. Norm, Jamie, Lily, and Lonnie were waiting when they arrived. Friends began gathering in the pews inside, and the flowers on the altar shimmered in the light.

Angie shook inside as Pastor Frank stood before her and Norm.

"Angie, Norm, friends, and family, this evening we're gathered together…" he began. The lights suddenly went out. O-U-T as in blackout.

Gathered together in a jet-black room. Oh great! Not so much as a street lamp. And the moon? Hiding behind a tree. God, please, let there be light. You've done it before.

Julia squeezed my hand. "Mom, what are we going to do now? Come back tomorrow?"

"I hope not, honey."

Pastor Frank groped his way off the platform and returned with two lit candles.

"Shall we keep going?"

Norm nodded yes and then looked at Angie.

She nodded and grabbed his hand. *This is not the romantic wedding I had in mind.* She glanced up at Norm and her heart swelled. *But maybe it's even more romantic this way.* He looked so handsome in the candlelight. His eyes shone and his hand felt good in hers. Angie breathed and steadied herself. *God, I do love this man. Help me to be the wife he deserves. I can't do it without you.*

Norm and Angie exchanged vows. They slipped gold bands onto each other's ring finger, and Pastor Frank pronounced them man and wife. Then the children and Norm and Angie promised out loud to uphold one another in their new family. They committed to love each other in sickness and in health, in riches and in poverty. And, as Angie looked around, in darkness and in light!

Reflection

You, O Lord, keep my lamp burning; my God
turns my darkness into light (Psalm 18:28).

Lord, thank you that your grace and your watchful eyes are enough to keep me safe in all my decisions and actions.

Something's Fishy

⸘⸙

Will stood at the kitchen counter and drummed his fingers. "Let's go! What's the hold-up?"

"Ready in a minute!" Renee shouted from the hall. "I can't find my fishing pole."

"It's in the car with the tackle box," Will called. "You put it there yourself last night. Don't you remember? You're not having a senior moment, are you?"

"If I'd remembered, I wouldn't be looking for it," Renee shot back, annoyed with herself and with her husband.

"For Pete's sake. By the time we arrive the fish will have gone to bed."

"Very funny, Mr. Seinfeld!"

They finally made it out to the car and took off. They drove in silence till they reached the turn-off for Lake Dorothy, a spot they'd heard was great for trout.

Renee sat forward and waved her right hand. "Turn left here. There. No, I mean here."

Will braked and the two jolted forward. "A little warning, please, especially in this weather. Looks like a storm is on the way."

"*You* missed the turn. Don't blame *me.*"

"Yes, *I* missed it." Will grabbed the map out of Renee's hand and traced the route himself.

Renee slumped, feeling stupid. *All our preparations and for what, Lord? It's miserable outside, and it's miserable in this car with you know who.*

Will parked. Renee grabbed her rain jacket and fishing gear, jumped out of the car, and strode briskly to the pier.

Renee heard Will's heavy footsteps coming up behind her. *I'll find my own fishing spot, thank you very much!* she thought.

"Careful," Will called. "The planks'll be pretty slippery from the rain. Renee, are you listening?"

Renee marched forward, head held high. Then suddenly she slipped! Tush down, feet up. Jacket askew. She burst into tears.

Lord, I can't keep track of my pole. Can't read a map. Can't walk without slipping. And I can't hold my own with Will.

She sat up, and there was her husband beside her, helping her to her feet, hugging her tight, brushing her hair back with his gentle hands. "Honey, are you hurt? When I saw you slip, I thought you were going right off the pier. My heart nearly drowned."

He straightened her jacket and kissed her head and linked his arm in hers. "Didn't you hear me warn you?"

Will's words tumbled in Renee's mind. *"Didn't you hear me warn you?"* Yes, I heard them, but I was too proud to heed them.

Renee turned and wrapped her arms around her husband. She held on so tight he nearly lost his balance. Then Renee stepped back and looked up at him. She saw relief in his blue eyes and felt his warm breath shield her face from the cold.

"Thanks for loving me," she said.

"Was there any doubt?"

"Maybe for a second or two." She smiled, picked up her pole, and reached for the bait. "Right now it's time to catch some fish."

"You've 'caught' me," Will joked.

"And *you've* hooked *me*," Renee responded. "Completely."

Reflection

Pride only breeds quarrels, but wisdom is found
in those who take advice (Proverbs 13:10).

———————

Pride! It gets me every time. Dear God, help me to hear you sooner rather than later. Spare my loved ones the sting of my hurtful words and cruel thoughts. Let me salvage the good and toss the bad.

PART 5

THOSE
GRANDKIDS

Breakfast Bonanza

Roger parked his van in the driveway of his parents' house. His sons, eight-year-old Jason and four-year-old Wally, tugged at their duffels and sleeping bags stuffed into the back of the rig. They hopped out of the van and ran up the walkway. Their dad grabbed them just before they rang the bell.

"Remember, boys, this is a *treat*. Grandma and Grandpa aren't as young as they used to be. Be on your best behavior, all right? No fussing when Grandma says it's bedtime, and you eat everything on your plate, you hear? Make your mom and me proud."

"We will, Dad, I promise," said Jason.

"Me too," echoed Wally.

The boys tore away from their dad when the door opened and Grandma and Grandpa spread their arms wide to greet them.

Roger hugged his parents and thanked them for taking the boys. "I've had a good talk with Jason and Wally. They know what I expect of them. I'll be looking for a clean report. Don't be afraid to discipline if needed."

"Roger, you and Jan go on now and have a good time. We raised you, and you turned out all right. I think we can handle two little boys for a weekend."

"Thanks," he said and hugged his sons and waved good-bye.

On Sunday afternoon Roger returned to pick up the boys. He was happy to hear they had gone to Sunday school and had eaten a hearty brunch. He picked up Wally and wiped off the crumbs from his mouth. "What'd you have, Little Buddy? Smells good in here."

Jason stepped in and answered for his younger brother. "We had calcium, protein, and fruit," he said proudly.

"Mom, what's this all about? Did you give them a lesson in basic nutrition?"

Roger walked into the kitchen and there on the counter was the evidence—a carton of ice cream, two banana peels, a package of crushed nuts, a squeeze bottle of chocolate syrup, and a jar of maraschino cherries!

"Grandma made us banana splits!" Wally volunteered.

"And we ate everything she put on our plates," said Jason, "just like you told us to, Dad."

Roger started to say something to his mother and then paused. "Sounds good to me," he said, winking at the boys. "Mom, got any calcium, protein, and fruit left over for *your* son?"

Reflection

You will have plenty to eat, until you are full, and
you will praise the name of the LORD your God
(Joel 2:26).

Lord, thank you for treats, for fun, for good times with family and friends. You never disappoint me. You not only provide for my needs, but you are my very portion.

Pickpocket

Gloria and her husband, Gil, like to tuck a dollar or a bit of change into their grandchildren's pockets now and again. "They love to buy their own ice cream cone or pick up a little toy," Gloria commented. "We didn't have much when we were kids, so we get a kick out of blessing Danny and Laura in this way."

The custom was well established when a younger sister came along. By the time baby Renee was three years old she knew a little about money and what she could do with it. In fact, she kept her grandmother hopping whenever they went grocery shopping together. As they strolled up and down each aisle and packed the cart with food and treats, Renee never failed to remind Gloria, "Before we go you have to pay."

"I guess she thought I was a thief in disguise," joked Gloria.

One day Gil had a roll of quarters and a few single dollars in his jeans pocket. "Who wants a bit of spending money?" he asked while he and the kids took a drive to a nearby mall.

"Me!" shouted eight-year-old Danny.

"Me too!" echoed his younger sister Laura.

"I want some!" squeaked Renee.

Gil wasn't sure the youngest child knew what it meant to have spending money, but he didn't want to leave her out, so he pulled out enough for all three.

He doled out three singles for Danny, three for Laura, and then he counted out 12 quarters for Renee and slipped them into her pocket for safekeeping. Renee, by that time aged four, wrinkled her brow and gave Gil a knowing look. She reached into her pocket, picked out the quarters, and gave them all back.

"What's this about?" Grandpa Gil asked. "You don't want to buy an ice cream or a toy?"

She took a deep breath. "Yes. But, Papa, I only like the green stuff."

Reflection

He who gathers money little by little makes
it grow (Proverbs 13:11).

———————

Lord, oh the wisdom and delight of little children! Even at a young age they are perceptive and wise, yet still they remain innocent. They tell it like it is. May I learn from them in order to draw closer to you.

Ho! Ho! Ho! Santa

Yolanda and her grandson Jacob chatted in the car as she drove
him to soccer practice one day in September. Jacob didn't
usually burst into song, but this day he was eager to share a
new piece of music he'd learned at school.

"Grandma!" he said with excitement. "Wanna hear a new
Christmas song I learned today?"

Yolanda was surprised the teacher was introducing holiday
music so soon. Why Labor Day had just passed, and they had
Halloween and Thanksgiving to think about next. But she didn't
want to discourage her grandson. "Sure," she said. "Let's hear it."

Jacob sat up straight, cleared his throat, and belted out, "Ho,
ho, ho, Santa. He died to save us from our sins. Ho, ho, ho, Santa.
He died to save both you and me."

Yolanda furrowed her brow and looked at her grandson. This
was one of the strangest Christmas songs she'd ever heard. And it
was theologically incorrect, to boot! *Hmmm.* "You sang that really
well, Jacob," she responded.

She swung into the parking lot next to the soccer field. Jacob got out and headed toward his team. Yolanda decided to call Jacob's mother to suggest she speak to the teacher about the song. After all, Jacob attended a Christian school. Just as she picked up her cell phone to dial, it suddenly hit her. "Hosanna!" she exclaimed "I'll bet Jacob heard the Ho! Ho! part and thought the rest of the phrase was Santa. Ho! Ho! Ho! Santa, instead of Ho-ho-hosanna!" She had a good laugh as she got out to watch the practice.

Reflection

Those who went ahead and those who followed
shouted, "Hosanna!" "Blessed is he who comes
in the name of the Lord!" (Mark 11:9).

God, I must surely cause you to smile sometimes with my little foibles and follies. And yet You love me with an everlasting love, always wanting the best for me. You're ever ready to bless my efforts even when I fall short or don't hear things just right. Thank You for loving me.

Sorry State

Silly me.
Couldn't help it.
Pardon me.
O dear!

Most of us have uttered such empty phrases or heard others express them to us. At the most they're lame; at the least they're insulting. Sincere apology over a sin against someone else takes more than a quick phrase and a fast exit. It requires us to humble ourselves before another person and truly get the hurt and pain we inflicted. Then it's up to us to repair the damage the best way we can by the grace of God.

I was reminded of this recently when my two-and-a-half-year-old grandson, Miles, asked for his treat after using the potty like a big boy. The customary reward was a couple of chocolate chips. I gave him three, and he closed his little hand around them. He then asked me to put them in a cup the way his mommy does.

I popped the chips into a blue plastic cup and handed it to him.

He asked for more. I gave him a couple extras. He asked for more again, and I said, "No, not just now. That's enough for today."

He stomped to the sink and turned the cup upside down, sending the chocolate chips into the drain. He stood his ground and pouted. I was shocked by this unexpected behavior.

"That wasn't nice," I said. I went about my business.

He followed me around the kitchen pulling on my pant leg and making ugly faces and weird grunts at me. I didn't recognize this side of a boy who is usually sweet and joyful. I ignored his attempts to taunt me and continued emptying the dishwasher.

Suddenly he left the room and joined his sisters watching television. Then back he came, asking for yogurt with chocolate chips on top.

"No. You hurt me when you threw the chocolate chips in the sink. I need to hear you're sorry before we can be okay with one another."

He left again. Then a moment later he returned and in his big boy voice he apologized: "Grammy, I'm sorry I got mad at you. And I'm sorry I dumped the chips in the sink."

I bent down to his level and reached out to him. "I forgive you." We hugged each other, and he helped me dish up the yogurt.

When his mother returned later that night he was quick to tattle on himself. "But I told Grammy I was sorry," he added.

His mother sat forward. "Then what happened?"

"She said, 'I forgive you.'"

"Now it's all better, right?" asked his mom.

Miles nodded and went off to play, a little wiser I hope. He learned what it meant to hurt someone with his anger and defiance, and I learned to ask for a well-deserved apology. Then we both discovered together the healing power of making up with forgiveness and a hug.

It's that way with God, too. He's quick to forgive when we apologize and repent in earnest. If you have something heavy on your heart, go to the Lord and confess. He'll fill your cup to over-flowing with love and forgiveness. Then you can move on fully restored.

Reflection

Now I am happy, not because you were made
sorry, but because your sorrow led you to
repentance (2 Corinthians 7:9).

———————

Lord, too often I behave like a self-centered toddler, hanging on to my position, my conviction, my wants despite how they affect other people. Please help me be quick to apologize, to repent, and to forgive so I can be right with you and with the other person.

Head in the Clouds

The summer my grandson Liam turned four I invited him on an overnight adventure at the San Diego Zoo Safari Park. We were going to tour the park with other adults and young children, enjoy a barbecue dinner, and sleep in tents on the lawn outside the animal enclosures. The next morning we'd have a buffet breakfast, a walk through the "dinosaur" kingdom, and then a bus ride before heading back to our cars.

An official park guide explained the rules to the group, emphasizing the importance of staying away from the fenced enclosures. "We don't want to lose anyone," she joked.

While waiting for one of the activities to begin, I sat down in front of our tent to relax for a moment. Suddenly I noticed Liam climbing the wire fence above the rhinoceros den. I jumped up. "Stop!" I shouted and ran toward the exhibit.

One of the guides beat me there. She grabbed him by the collar and yanked him off the fence. I could tell she was both annoyed and concerned, especially since she had just given her pep talk on safety.

When she admonished him tactfully about the perils of falling into the pit below, he looked up at her as though she didn't have a clue about whom she was talking to.

"Ms. Diane," he said politely but firmly. "It's okay if I fall in. I'm wearing my Nikes, and I can run faster than any big old rhinoceros."

Reflection

Let us run with perseverance the race marked out for us (Hebrews 12:1).

Lord, sometimes I get it into my head that I'm faster, smarter, wiser than I am. I want to scale mountains, swim across mighty rivers, and charge ahead of a wild animal—without thinking of the consequences. Thank You for reminding me that living for You requires more than sheer will power and determination. It requires humility, perseverance, and obedience over the long haul.

Ice Queen

⋘⟨⟨ ⟩⟩⋙

Betty turned the pages of an old photo album while gliding on the swing on her front porch. She fingered one picture of her and her father waltzing across the frozen pond by the family home when she was around eight. She remembered that day vividly. Dad had given up a Saturday morning on the farm to go skating with her for her birthday—the one gift she'd wanted.

Betty teared up when she looked at the stocking cap and gloves she was wearing. Her mother had given them to her that day so she'd stay warm while she skated. Later Betty and her dad returned home and curled up together in front of the fireplace and sipped hot chocolate and ate glazed donuts.

The phone rang, interrupting Betty's reverie. She laid the album on the glass side table and answered the call on the second ring. She was expecting to hear from her granddaughter Carrie. She listened for a moment and then spoke up. "All right, darling. I'll be there, but just for your birthday lunch, okay? I can't skate with you and your friends afterward. It's been years since I've even put on a pair of skates. I'll sit on the bench and cheer you on."

"But, Grams, you have to skate!" begged Carrie. "All my friends want to see you on the ice. It'll be fun. I'll hold your hand if you get scared. Besides the ice rink is really safe. No bumps…and there's a guy in a vest who skates around to make sure no one gets hurt."

Betty sighed and murmured a prayer, *Lord, did you set this up? Okay, I'll do it but I'm going to need one of your angel bodyguards.* Betty agreed to skate, and Carrie whooped with joy.

The following Saturday Betty met Carrie and her mother and Carrie's friends at the Westside Indoor Skating Rink. They ate lunch at the ringside tables and then went to the room where everyone changed into rental skates. They walked to the rink. As Betty stepped onto the ice her heart was pounding hard and her hands were sweaty with worry. She held on to the sideboard as she half-skated and half-walked around the rink. The second time she let go of the board and grasped Carrie's hand instead. By the third time her confidence returned, and she felt like a young girl again. She skated out to the center of the rink and began making figure eights on the ice.

Then she did something she hadn't done in years. She held up one leg and steadied herself on the other, arms outstretched—but not for long. The next thing Betty knew she was flat on her backside, feet up in the air. *How embarrassing!* Carrie and her friends rushed over to check on her. "You all right, Grams?" Carrie pulled Betty to her feet.

Just then the kid in the orange vest with STAFF printed across the front zoomed over and asked if Betty needed a doctor or an aspirin or an ambulance. He sounded scared.

Betty didn't like attention, but this kind of attention was the worst kind. "I'm fine," she muttered. "My granddaughter said her friends wanted to see me on ice, and I didn't want to disappoint them."

Reflection

Be strong and take heart, all you who hope in
the Lord (Psalm 31:24).

———————

Lord, I'm so thankful I can participate in life, regardless of the little mishaps.

Dot Org

know a thing or two about computers and about websites. I've been in business for 35 years, and I feel good about my technical skills, given that I started with a manual typewriter and transitioned up to the latest Mac. I can Google, cut-and-paste, create an alias file, and retrieve a "lost" document with the best of 'em. But I can be knocked off my office chair by a four-year-old who will soon pass me by—perhaps even before he learns to read.

A few weeks ago my grandson came to visit. One of his favorite pastimes is to play on my computer. I have games and puzzles and cartoons, all kinds of fun stuff to entertain him for an hour at least. He knows the rules. No playing on the computer unless I'm with him. Being careful and gentle with the equipment. Following my instructions when a problem arises. With tech consulting and repair fees running more than $100 an hour, I don't want to risk him disabling or erasing some important program or messing with the system. So far so good.

I sat him on my lap during that visit, and he asked to play some games his sisters knew about on a particular website. I was familiar with what he wanted, but I couldn't remember the URL. I typed in a couple of different ones, hoping my mind would kick in and provide at least a hint. After a couple of minutes of listening to me saying, "Nope. Not yet. Haven't got it quite right. One more try…" Miles folded his arms across his chest and let out a big sigh. And there was no mistaking the tone of disgust that went with it.

"Grammy," the little one piped up in a loud voice, "PBSKIDS DOT O-R-G."

He got my attention. I typed it in and—presto!—we reached the portal to the games he wanted.

Sure enough, the golden years ain't for wimps! To keep up with four-year-old tech-savvy grandchildren one has to muster on or be set aside.

Reflection

Faith is being sure of what we hope for and
certain of what we do not see (Hebrews 11:1).

———————

Dear God, thank you that I can learn from the children in my life, just as they can learn from me…and I can learn from you.

Chinny Chin Chin

⌒⊙⊙⌒

Gail leaned in toward the hand mirror and looked at her face. She turned it over to the magnifying side. A little better, but it was still hard to see as close as she wanted to. And she really wanted to see up close now that she was prone to a brand-new condition she wasn't prepared for.

The hair that used to be on her legs had suddenly sprouted on her chin…and some of the little buggers were black and curly, even though the hair on her head was more white than gray. Her granddaughter Queenie had alerted her to the malady one autumn day when the two were having a picnic in the backyard. As Gail cut the peanut butter and jelly sandwiches into little squares and placed them in front of the four-year-old, Queenie piped up in a loud voice. "Grams, why do you have a black curl on your chin? Mom doesn't have one."

Gail ran a finger over her chin where Queenie pointed and sure enough, something pointy was sticking out of her smooth skin. She ran inside, grabbed a hand mirror, and inspected her face inch by inch. There it was. A black curly hair jutting straight out. Gail wondered how long it had been there. How had she missed it? Had the clerk at the grocery store noticed? Did the sight of it turn her husband away? Did her best friend, Ruth, laugh behind her back? She imagined the worst.

Gail fished for her tweezers and pulled that puppy out by its black tail and tossed it into the trash. She couldn't eat a bite till it was out of her life.

Just when she'd started enjoying the fact that she wouldn't have to shave her legs or underarms but once every couple of months, here she was on the verge of growing a beard. Next thing she knew she might be borrowing her husband's razor.

Gail dragged herself back to the picnic table, and she and Queenie ate their sandwiches. But Gail's mind was elsewhere. She couldn't stop thinking about the potential invasion of black hairs on her white chin. She considered electrolysis. Painful procedure, she'd heard, but it was now or never when it came to the invaders. Get 'em while she still had control. Like weeds in the garden, one can't wait too long or they take over the flowerbed.

"Grams?" Queenie interrupted Gail's thoughts. "What are you thinking about? You look sad."

Gail patted her granddaughter's soft hand. "It's hard to get old, honey. First the wrinkles land and now the black hairs pop out. And worst of all, I didn't notice them till you told me."

Queenie climbed off the picnic bench and tucked her little body next to her grandmother's on the other side of the table. She petted Gail's face and looked at her with soulful eyes. "One black hair doesn't matter. All of the rest of your face is beautiful."

Reflection

No weapon forged against you will prevail
(Isaiah 54:17).

Dear God, I know you don't love me based on looks, but it sure feels nice when I do look good. Help me always do my best to reflect the best you've made me to be.

Bread and Jam

Lydia woke up early on Monday morning. She stayed in bed a bit longer than usual so she could look again at the cards and notes and letters stacked on her bedside table from her birthday party the previous Saturday night. The number of people who wished her a happy ninetieth nearly matched the number of candles on the cake her granddaughter Mandy had made from scratch—a New York-style cheesecake to commemorate Lydia's city of birth nearly a century before.

She sat up and dangled her legs over the side of the bed, thinking back over her long life. At the same time Lydia felt a bit dismayed. She wasn't sure she deserved all this attention. She'd lived a good clean life and that was that. No need to make a big deal out of it. She got where she'd gotten because of the grace of God, and because she contended for the long life that he promises to those who love and obey him. She didn't see why reaching 90 was any more deserving of a celebration than reaching 10 or 32 or 67.

It was nice, though, to reread the prayers and wishes of her family and friends who had stopped to write. Some had even come by on Sunday afternoon to kiss and hug her in person and enjoy a piece of the cheesecake decorated with fresh flowers from Mandy's garden. The lemon-mint tea with just a dollop of honey was lovely too. It had been her favorite flavor ever since she could remember.

As for the cheesecake, well it was good of Mandy to take the time to make it. After all she had three young children to take care of. It's not as if she had hours to spare making a fuss over an old lady. But cheesecake just wasn't high on Lydia's enjoyable foods list. She debated about letting Mandy know her feelings on the matter. Since her granddaughter had gone to so much effort, why didn't she go a step further and make a lemon chiffon cake or a double fudge chocolate or a pecan crunch with French vanilla frosting or…

The doorbell stopped her in her thoughts. "Coming," she called as she padded softly to the front door in her new faux fur-lined slippers.

It was Mandy! "Hello, darlin,'" Lydia said, embracing her granddaughter as the women walked into the kitchen. "What brings you by? Whatever it is, I'm glad to see you."

"Just checking up on you, Grammy. You all right? You had a lot of excitement over the weekend." She walked to the counter and touched the cake dish that held the remains of the huge cheese-cake she'd made. "I thought you'd have finished this off by now," Mandy joked.

Lydia couldn't lie. But she didn't know how to tell the truth either—given this delicate situation. She hesitated.

"Grammy, is something going on?" Mandy wrinkled her brow.

"I'm afraid you wasted your money and your time on the cheesecake, much as I appreciate all that you did to honor me."

"Grammy, it was my pleasure. Don't you know how much I love and admire you?"

Lydia cleared her throat and braced herself against the counter. "I do indeed. That's why it's hard to admit what I think I should."

"And what is that?"

"Well, dear," Lydia said in the sweetest tone she could muster, "the cake filling is as smooth and tasty as butter itself, but the only way I can eat butter is between two halves of a hot biscuit with strawberry jam on top!"

Mandy laughed so hard Lydia was afraid she'd fall over. "Oh, Grammy, you do take the cake," said Mandy. "Pardon the pun! Thanks for telling me cheesecake isn't your favorite. It's okay."

After a few closing words, the women hugged goodbye and Mandy slipped out the door with a wave.

The next morning the doorbell rang just as Lydia was about to sit down to a cup of lemon-mint tea with a teaspoonful of honey. It was her granddaughter—again!

"Here you go, Grammy," she said, a twinkle in her eye indicating a bit of mischief up her sleeve. She handed Lydia a bag.

Lydia opened it and gasped. Nestled in bakery tissue paper were two golden biscuits, warm from the oven, and a miniature jar of strawberry jam.

"Just a little something to go with your cheesecake butter," she said and then planted a kiss on Lydia's forehead. "Enjoy!" With that she slipped out the door again, and Lydia sat down to enjoy the treat.

Turning 90 definitely had its plus side. She could speak up, be heard, and even better, have her wishes granted!

Reflection

The cheerful heart has a continual feast
(Proverbs 15:15).

Lord, how nice to be able to speak the truth and have it received in the spirit in which I offer it.

Never Too Late

Steppin' out is exactly what my grandson Noah and I have done over the course of his growing-up years. We both love the outdoors. We like to skitter over rocks, hike in the mountains, explore caves, and even climb trees.

When Noah was eight I took him to the desert for a youth campout. I packed individual bags of snacks so we'd never go hungry. My grandson loved being able to go to the car whenever he felt like it to help himself to goodies. I didn't place any restrictions on him. I wanted him to have plenty of energy for all the activities we'd planned.

One night as we lay in our tent under the stars, we gazed through the net roof and pondered the beautiful gifts of nature that God had created for us.

"Magah" (his pet name for me), Noah said with a catch in his voice, "I could stay here forever. At home I get bored with video games and my bike and the computer. But there's so much to do here. I'd never get bored! I could climb that hill all day every day, couldn't you?"

Not exactly! But I got what he was saying. It's just that I didn't have quite the stamina at 58 that he had at age 8. Still I wanted to affirm his perspective on what really mattered.

"I love the quiet," he added. "It's so peaceful here."

I knew just what he meant. It was holy ground. We could feel the touch of God in every rock and tree and flower and animal.

Next it was my turn to choke up.

As we hiked around the hills the following day, I said, "Noah, someday I won't be able to do this. I'll be too old. I don't want that day to come. I love being here with you. It's so special."

Quickly Noah came back with the most beautiful response.

"Don't you worry, Magah," he said tenderly. "When you're too old I'll just sling you over my shoulder and hike up to the top so you can look at this all over again."

Reflection

May the LORD bless his land with the choicest
gifts of the ancient mountains and the fruitfulness
of the everlasting hills (Deuteronomy 33:13, 15).

Lord, how good it is to hang out in nature, enjoying the gifts of your creation and sharing them with others who appreciate what you have done. Thank you for oceans and streams, trees and flowers, meadows and mountains.

PART 6

AGING PARENTS

Snip, Snip!

❦

One day Margaret's daughter Ruth called. "Mom, we're having our annual family photo on Saturday at Nobel Park. We all hope you're up for it. Mick and I will pick you up at one o'clock sharp. If you need help dressing or getting ready, let me know and I'll come early. And one more thing. We'll be having a picnic afterward, so bring your appetite. By the way, Will and Jordan will be there with their girlfriends. It's looking serious between Will and Lynn. I can't wait till you meet Lynn."

"Tsk tsk." Margaret was known to "tst tsk" whenever her two grandsons brought new girlfriends around. She wished they'd each pick one, settle down, get married, and give her some great-grandchildren before it was too late. At age 82 she figured she was at heaven's gate.

She agreed to the photo shoot and said she could manage on her own quite nicely. No help needed—at least not yet.

The following Saturday Ruth and Mick met Margaret at her

front door. The entire family met at the park. Within an hour the professional photographer was done. Margaret held up her hand. "I'd like a few with my camera," she announced.

Ruth stepped forward. "But Mom, we can get you copies of the ones we just had taken."

"I'd like my own," Margaret asserted. "If you don't mind."

"All right. But I don't see the point." Ruth was clearly agitated with her mother's insistence.

"Get back into formation," Ruth called to everyone. "One more photo for Mom with her camera."

Adults, children, and teens murmured among themselves and gathered reluctantly. Margaret took over. She lined up each person in the order she preferred.

Will wrinkled his brow. Jordan grabbed Amy's hand and pulled her close to him in the second row.

"Lynn and Amy, you move to the ends—one on each side," shouted Margaret, waving her hands and pointing to the spots where she wanted the girlfriends to stand.

Ruth pulled her mother aside. "What's this all about? You're creating a lot of confusion."

Margaret leaned in and whispered to her daughter. "I put the girlfriends on the end so if it doesn't work out between them and the boys—and it probably won't—I'll take the photo and snip, snip."

Reflection

Do not be anxious about anything
(Philippians 4:6).

Lord, this is funny—more so because I can relate to it. I see girlfriends and boyfriends coming and going in young peoples' lives, and I want to hold up a sign that says: Caution! Commitment ahead! But I must step aside and allow them to lead their own lives, covering them with my love and prayers.

Coffee, Anyone?

Nonie loved coffee, but coffee didn't love her. In fact it gave her cramps. The acid content was a bit much for her stomach. Since her reaction on some days was better than on others, she took her chances. She couldn't help but indulge. Nonie loved the aroma, the deep color, and the curl of steam rising over her favorite cup of brew. With a bit of honey and a splash of half and half, she was in heaven.

Nonie's daughter Laurie had a decidedly different opinion of coffee—especially when it came to her 83-year-old mother. She had spoken to her mom over and over about this coffee addiction and the fact that she, Laurie, was the one to rush over to her mother's apartment with antacid pills whenever Nonie had one cup too many.

Laurie decided to take matters into her own hands. For Mother's Day she purchased a beautiful pink Brown Betty teapot, a matching set of cups, and a basket of assorted herbal teas:

Chamomile, Lotus Blossom, Red Zinger, and, most important, Echinacea Wellness tea.

"Mom, I want you to promise me you'll try to exchange the coffee habit for the tea habit." Then Laurie launched into a lecture on the merits of the various selections. "Chamomile before bed assures a sweet sleep, and Echinacea Wellness will support your immune system and all-around good health."

Nonie listened patiently but Laurie could tell her mother was not buying her spiel. She'd always been stubborn, and she didn't appear to be any less so as she grew older.

The next time the two visited, they sat in the den—Nonie in her favorite recliner, and Laurie on the sofa across the room.

"Mom, how are you feeling? Any better?"

Nonie clutched her stomach. "Fair."

Laurie let out a deep breath and faced her mother eye-to-eye. "Are you still drinking coffee?" she asked. "After all I've told you and after I went to the trouble of buying you a beautiful teapot and cups and selecting delicious teas that will actually help you feel better?"

Nonie lowered her head. "Yes. I can't break the habit. When I go too long without a cup I get this terrible headache."

"And when you drink it, you get a stomachache. Which is worse?"

Nonie closed her eyes and rested her head against the chair.

Laurie stood up and paced the room. "Mom, this cannot go on! What am I going to do with you?" She thought for a moment and then tried a new tactic. "Mother, what do you think God wants you to do about this addiction that is hurting your body, which is his temple?" Laurie was sure she was on to something that would work. She knew how much her mother loved the Lord and that she wanted to please him above anyone else. "I think we should pray about this together and read God's Word for guidance."

Laurie reached for her mother's Bible on the bookshelf above the sofa.

Nonie raised her hand. "I've already done all that," she said. "I'm sure the Lord is fine with me drinking coffee. There is nothing in the Bible against it."

Laurie sighed. She was sure her mother was right. She couldn't imagine there being any reference to coffee in God's Word. But that wasn't the point. She wanted to focus on helping her mother pray for wisdom and strength so she could give up what was clearly not working.

Nonie stood up, walked to the sofa, and plucked the Bible out of Laurie's hands. She turned quickly to the New Testament and then lay the book open to the page she'd looked for.

"The Bible doesn't say anything against coffee," she said. "But it does seem to refer to it in a positive way."

Laurie frowned. She feared her mother was losing it.

"It's right here," said Nonie. "*He brews.*"

Reflection

Surely you desire truth in the inner parts;
you teach me wisdom in the inmost place
(Psalm 51:6).

———

Lord, what fun to play with words and know you enjoy my sense of humor!

Who's in My Bed?

❦

Bonnie set her teacup down and turned to her husband. "I know it's a challenge, Ralph, but I want to keep Mom and Dad home with us as long as possible. Are you with me on this?"

Ralph let out a deep breath and glanced at the photo of his in-laws on the wall above the kitchen table. "Of course I'm with you. But it's hard to believe they're the same people in this picture. So much has changed in the last ten years. It makes me sad."

Bonnie reached across the table and patted his hand. "I know what you mean. Are we heading down the same path?"

"I don't want to think about it." Ralph drained his coffee cup and pushed himself away from the table.

Bonnie turned at the sound of footsteps in the hallway. She knew it was her father, now up for the day and probably looking for his coffee and toast—the same breakfast he'd eaten for the past 50 years. Her mother, Jean, would soon follow. Bonnie knew her mom was devoted to looking after her husband now that his memory was slipping and he wasn't as steady on his feet as he used to be.

Bonnie noticed her dad seemed agitated. She hoped she could communicate with him enough to calm him down. She worried that he wouldn't recognize her. One day he'd call her Bonnie, and the next he'd call her Olive, the name of his older sister, whom he'd always loved and looked up to. Sure enough, today Bonnie was "Olive" to her dad.

"Olive! Olive!" he called. Bonnie could tell he was frantic with worry.

"I'm here." She met him in the hall and linked her arm in his. "Right this way. Your coffee and toast are ready."

Ben shook his head and waved her away, nearly smacking Bonnie in the face, though it was clear he didn't know what he was doing.

"What is it? You look frightened." She helped him into a chair.

"There was a strange woman in bed with me. Nearly scared the daylights out of me. Get her out of here! What will your mother think?"

Bonnie covered her mouth to keep from laughing out loud. "That's your wife and my mom, Jean. The same woman you've been married to for 63 years."

"I don't believe it. She looks different. Jean has blond hair and blue eyes. She doesn't wear glasses, and she's skinny too."

Just then Bonnie saw her mother come around the corner and into the kitchen. Bonnie hoped her mom hadn't heard her father's hurtful remark.

"What'd I tell you, Olive!" Ben shouted when Jean sat down next to him. "Now will you believe me?" He pointed to the stranger. "This woman has gray hair and glasses and she's plump."

Bonnie grabbed her mother's trembling hand and squeezed it. "Daddy's teasing." She hoped to ease the tension in the room, but it didn't work.

Jean looked at Bonnie and then at Ben. "He's right," she said and chuckled. "I don't know this man, and he doesn't know me. My husband has brown hair, a mustache, gray eyes, and strong muscles."

Bonnie cracked up. Ralph broke out laughing, and Bonnie's parents joined in.

Ralph winked at Bonnie. "Looks like we have some shopping to do."

"Shopping?" Bonnie wondered if her husband was losing it too. What did shopping have to do with her parents' confusion?

He patted his back pocket, which held his wallet. "We'll have to buy separate beds for these two and put them in different rooms. Can't have strangers sleeping with one another in our house."

Bonnie let out a sigh and smiled. It wouldn't be easy, but with Ralph at her side she could handle anything—even the surprising and sometimes amusing changes in her parents.

Reflection

My flesh and my heart may fail, but God is the
strength of my heart and my portion forever
(Psalm 73:26).

———————

*I love you, Lord, and I know you love me. Thank you
for being with me in the trials and triumphs of life.*

Now Hear This

M om and Dad visit us every summer," Emily shared. "They arrive on Memorial Day weekend and stay through Labor Day. I have loved these extended times together, but as the years pass, things are changing. They just don't hear as well as they used to."

Emily and her husband, Roy, decided to do something about it. They were frustrated with having to repeat themselves. It also bothered them that Emily's parents couldn't hear each other. "What'd you say?" "Speak louder." "Can't get it. Say it again." These became stock phrases around their home.

One day Emily took matters into her own hands. "Mom and Dad," she announced, "today Roy and I are taking you out to buy top-of-the-line hearing aids. It's an early Christmas present to you," she said smiling. "And one to us!" she added under her breath.

The four made the rounds, and then settled on a store that sold exactly what they were hoping for. The older couple was fitted for the aids, and Roy paid for them. Afterward they went to lunch to celebrate. Emily was relieved to know that now even in a noisy restaurant she and her mother could converse without questioning looks and misunderstandings.

They arrived at Sheldon's Deli for their favorite corned beef sandwiches on rye with a dill pickle on the side. Her mom and dad slid into one side of the booth, and Emily and Roy took the other side.

Margie, the server, approached their table and passed out menus. They placed their order, and Margie went off to fill it.

Emily leaned over to her mother and asked how the hearing aids felt: "Do you notice a difference?"

Her mother winked. "Oh yes. They're working so well, I can almost hear your thoughts!"

Emily laughed. She appreciated her mother's sense of humor. She was taking this symptom of old age in stride. Emily hoped she'd be as gracious when her time came.

The server arrived and set out the sandwiches. Then she passed out the drinks: a strawberry malt for Emily, lemonade for Emily's mom, and iced tea for the men.

Emily noticed her mother looking around for something. "What do you need, Mom?"

"Please pass the salt."

Emily smiled and pushed her malt across the table. She was happy to share a sip with her mother.

"Salt, dear. S-A-L-T," her mother repeated in a loud voice.

"Sorry, Mom. What? Say that again."

Her mother mimicked pouring salt. "SALT," she called, cupping her mouth with her hands. Then she pointed to her hearing aid. "No worries, Emily. I know just what you need, and I now know where to get it!"

Emily wanted to slide under the table. "You got me there, Mom," she admitted as she sipped her malt—and passed the salt.

Reflection

Bring me any case too hard for you, and I will
hear it (Deuteronomy 1:17).

———————

Lord, aren't I the know-it-all sometimes? Impatient with the shortcomings of others—even my own parents—until I see how imperfect I am. Thanks for listening, dear God, and for speaking so clearly that I get it with or without hearing aids.

Go Fish

Loretta's dad, Joe, came to live with her and her husband, Ron, when Joe turned 85. By that age he needed extra help, and Loretta felt more comfortable having him with her than on his own. He was also a big help. He fed the dog and fish, and he kept the flowers in the yard fertilized and watered.

One day at a local fair in town, Joe won a goldfish. He was tickled with his new pet. He took the little fellow home in a plastic bag filled with water. No need for a fishbowl, he decided. He'd just add the new fish to the bowl already on the kitchen counter. But when he saw how aggressive the first fish was toward the new goldfish he went to a local pet store to inquire about this behavior.

"What kind of fish is the first one?" the clerk asked.

"An Oscar," Joe answered.

The clerk laughed. "That explains it." He pointed to the feeding instructions on the tank holding Oscars: "Favorite food—goldfish."

Joe didn't know what was so funny. He knew just what to do to take care of the problem. He thanked the clerk for setting him straight and off he went to the grocery store. He marched right down the aisle displaying crackers and cookies. "Yep, here's just the ticket," he muttered to himself. He picked up two packages of Goldfish crackers, paid for them, and walked home.

That night Ron asked Joe if he knew anything about the mush accumulated at the bottom of the fishbowl. Joe was in charge of feeding the fish and cleaning the tank.

"Oh *that*," Joe replied. "I found out at the pet store that Oscars' favorite food is goldfish so I picked up a couple of packages at the market."

Ron jumped up, grabbed a cup, and pulled out the *real* goldfish and put it into a bowl of its own. It was a close call!

Joe scratched his head. He still didn't see what all the fuss was about.

Reflection

Rule over the fish of the sea and the birds of the
air and over every living creature that moves on
the ground (Genesis 1:28).

———————

*Lord, sometimes I do the darndest things—even with
the best of intentions. It's a good thing there are people around to keep me in line. And even better is the
knowledge that You will enlighten my confused thinking with the power of your Word.*

Joy Ride

On's mother is 81. When he and his wife, Roxanne, visit her, they generally drive their Honda Gold Wing motorcycle from San Diego where they live, to Don's mother's house in Santa Cruz.

"During a recent visit," said Don, "I could tell Mom wanted to say something. But whenever I asked her if she was okay or if she had something on her mind, she brushed me off with 'I'm fine.' So I let it go. Then on Sunday after church she finally spoke up and asked me to take her for a ride on my motorcycle. What a surprise! She had told me to be careful so many times that I thought she hated the sight of it. She seemed terrified I'd kill myself. Now here she was practically begging me to take her on a joy ride.

"My wife grabbed Mom's kitchen step stool, and we helped her into the seat behind mine, put my wife's helmet on her, and buckled her in. Then off we went for a short ride around her neighborhood. Mom squealed like a teenager.

"'Now I see why you love this so much,' she said over and over. It was a kick to listen to her. I could only imagine the look on her face."

After Don and his mother returned, his mom asked if he'd take her on a ride along the ocean the next day.

"Once more we got out the step stool, loaded her up, and off we went. I don't know if I've ever seen my mother so carefree. It was fun for me to watch. Now I know where I get my young-at-heart attitude about life."

The following day Don and his wife and mother said goodbye. "I could tell Mom hated to see us leave," said Don. "If she were a few years younger, I think she'd have been ready to purchase a Gold Wing of her own. But then *I'd* be the one to shout, 'Be careful! You hear me?'"

A few weeks later Don invited his mother to visit him and his wife in San Diego. "Will you pick me up on the motorcycle?" she asked.

Don laughed out loud. "Mom," he said, "I'm not sure you're ready for *that*. An eight-hour drive on a saddle seat is not the same as a casual ride along the beach for a half hour."

"All right, I understand," she said. "But when I get there, will you take me for a ride around the block a few times?"

"Even more than a few, Mom—as many as you want."

Reflection

I will bless them and the places surrounding
my hill (Ezekiel 34:26).

Lord, what fun it is to kick back and enjoy the wind in my hair and the sun in my face, whether I'm riding around town on a motorcycle or napping in the hammock in my backyard. You have sent showers of blessings into my life! I want to enjoy every one of them with the people I love.

Driving Miss Lucy

Lucy is the first to admit that she has great faith in God…and her driving attests to it. Well into her eighties, she is now required to take a driver's test each year in August. She begins praying about it in January. Her daughter Joan does not agree with her mother in prayer. Not that she wants to deny her mom's freedom, but Lucy's eyesight, hearing, sense of direction, and reflexes aren't the best anymore.

Lucy is sharp as a tack mentally, but also stubborn as a mule—according to Joan. "Before the required insurance and seat belt laws ten years ago, Mom at age 76, drove her 20-year-old Mustang 40 miles on the freeway to her dying sister's house every day for three years.

"We had plenty of arguments about her cruising with the semis in rush hour traffic, but to no avail. She'd shrug her shoulders, shake her pretty white-haired head, and comment, 'I say a prayer when I put my key in the door lock and the good Lord takes care of me!'"

But then Lucy was in an accident. However, that didn't stop her from looking ahead. "When are we going to shop for a new car?" she asked Joan from the gurney in the hospital where she was rushed after her collision.

"Never!" Joan replied emphatically.

"Okay. I forgot to wear my seat belt, and it was dark, and I didn't see the car coming at me. That's all. No biggie."

"No biggie?" Joan shouted. "Mom, you totaled three cars! Your Mustang literally took flight into a parked car which 'dominoed' into another parked car demolishing all three!"

"I don't know what you're talking about," said Lucy. "All I know is that I don't have a car! So when are we going to get one?"

"Mom, your driving days are over," Joan said after a long silence. "You're not going to get your license back. You had restrictions, remember? No driving at night, glasses required, and of course a seat belt at all times."

"How do you feel, ma'am?" the emergency room doctor asked Lucy.

"Fine, fine. Not a thing hurts! Just my poor car. Can you do anything about that?"

Reflection

Some trust in chariots and some in horses, but
we trust in the name of the LORD, our God
(Psalm 20:7).

———————

Dear Lord, it's a challenge to give up our independence,
especially when it comes to driving. We are so used to

chauffeuring ourselves around town. How can we go back to buses and cabs and rides with friends and family when we long for the freedom to come and go as we wish when we wish? Help us to surrender peacefully and cooperatively when the time comes. With you at our side, we will be able to do all things in love—including giving up the wheel.

City Drivers

ook at these New York drivers!" Bob bellowed as he drove
down a familiar city street, chauffeuring his wife, son, and
daughter-in-law to a favorite restaurant. "They don't know
the first thing about safe driving."

Peter, Bob's son, sat in the rear seat, gripping the back of the
driver's seat with white knuckles. Peter had offered to drive, but
Bob would have none of it. Bob was proud of his new Buick, and
he wanted to show it off—as well as prove to his son that at age 81
he could still drive well.

"I don't see a problem with the New York drivers," Peter
remarked. "Seems like traffic is flowing nicely."

Bob turned to respond.

"Eyes on the road, please, Pop. I can hear you just fine," Peter
said. He felt his pulse rise with his voice. Suddenly, Peter realized
that the car was cruising faster than was safe. He shouted, "Pop,
brakes! Quick! Can't you see how close you are to the car in front
of you?"

"Dang city drivers!" Bob shouted. "Why don't they slow down when it's time to stop instead of slamming on their brakes and blinding me with their red lights?"

Peter took a deep breath. "Look, Pop. Brakes protect us. They're used in normal traffic and in fast stops when there isn't time to slow down gradually."

"You know how I feel about brakes," muttered Bob. "They're made to fail; that's what I think. Did I ever tell you about the time my brakes locked and…"

"Pop, that was 40 years ago," Peter reminded his father. "Cars are safer now. Brakes are tested…"

Peter didn't finish his sentence because once again, Bob was coming up too quickly on the car in front of them. His son was certain they were going to collide.

Whew! Another close call, Peter thought. He was sweating now. His father refused to use the brakes except an emergency. And when he was forced to use them, he believed the other driver had forced him into it.

The family arrived at their destination—a French cafe where they had planned a nice lunch. But as they settled into their booth, Peter realized he'd lost his appetite. He watched Bob yawning and his eyes blinking sleepily.

"Pop," he asked, "how about taking a snooze in the backseat while I drive us home? You deserve a *brake!*"

"Very funny," Bob replied, but he took Peter up on the offer.

They got home safe and sound. Peter let out a long breath as they pulled into the driveway—and then it was *his* turn to take a nap!

Reflection

I will instruct you and teach you in the way you should go; I will counsel you and watch over you (Psalm 32:8).

Dear Lord, I can imagine that some of our shenanigans here on earth bring you a smile or maybe a cringe. Some things that are so important to us are so unimportant in the big picture—but you love us in spite of our pettiness and small worries. Thank you for doing so. I need every bit of love you have for me.

Soaking Beauty

Louann's mother, Mabel, a retired hairstylist, always took pride in washing her own hair using the same long hose in her beautician's sink that she used with her many clients. However, Mabel's 89 years and her arthritic fingers made it difficult for her to continue the practice. According to Louann, "Mom's too proud to admit she needs help so I suggested an alternative." Louann was sure it would work for her mother as it did for her.

"Mom," she suggested, "have you tried washing your hair in the shower?"

"Yes," Mabel snapped, "and it was awful. I couldn't breathe. Water and shampoo ran all over my face. I thought I was drowning!"

Louann put a hand to her mouth to hide the smile that broke across her face.

"Mother," she said softly, "did you *face* the showerhead?"

"Well, of course. I leaned right into it. Anything wrong with that?" Mabel was clearly insulted by these elementary questions.

"Mom, next time, put your back to the showerhead and lean

back. The water will slide down your hair, and you can shampoo and rinse without a drop touching your eyes!"

"Oh! Now why didn't I think of that?" Mabel chirped.

The two had a good laugh and a big hug. Gettin' older just got easier for mom and daughter.

Reflection

Help the weak, be patient with everyone
(1 Thessalonians 5:14).

Dear God, as we grow older it's hard to admit we could use an extra hand. We like our independence. We want to keep on keeping on by ourselves, thank you very much! But when we must rely on others, help us embrace what you have provided through a trusted friend or relative or maybe even a kind stranger.

Heavenly Hotel

L aura, Mitch, come here, please." Iris called her son and daughter-in-law to her bedside in the nursing home. "Pretty soon I'll be gone, and I want to be sure you know my wishes before I go."

Mitch patted his mother's soft hand. "Mom, you can relax. Laura and I have everything written down. I promise we'll take care of all the details exactly the way you want us to. Please relax."

He glanced at the wall over his mother's bed. It was filled with framed acknowledgments of her many accomplishments over the 94 years of her life. She had completed college—the first in her family of seven siblings to do so—and had gone on for a master's degree in education. She had served as the president of the Women's Auxiliary at the local hospital, and one year had been voted Volunteer of the Year for spearheading a reading program for underprivileged children.

"Mom, you've done it all, and you were a great mother, as well.

We love you." Mitch leaned over and kissed her frail face. He felt tears well in his eyes as he realized any visit could be his last.

Iris was not one for sentiment, so she went back to her list of do's and don'ts for her funeral. Mitch snapped to attention as he repeated her wishes.

"I have a lot of friends here in Phoenix, some are gone, but there are still plenty, so have the funeral here in town. Then ship my body to Minneapolis where Hal and Ben are buried. I want to be in the same plot with my two husbands. Bless their souls, I wonder what they'd think of sharing me! Guess we'll never know." She laughed at the thought.

Iris sat forward and looked first at Mitch and then at Laura. "Listen carefully, please. Now, when we arrive in Minnesota for the second funeral service, I'll stay with the Petersons and you and your family will be in a motel. Might be wise to decide now where you want to stay so you won't be stuck at the last moment."

Laura looked at Mitch. They both grinned. "Mother, one nice thing about it being *your* funeral, you won't have to stay with the Petersons or worry about where we stay," said Laura.

Iris laughed out loud as she realized what she'd said. "Oh my, you're right, Laura! I'll be staying with Jesus. He said he's preparing a place for me."

"Right, Mom, and it will be perfect."

Reflection

Come, you who are blessed by my Father; take
your inheritance, the kingdom prepared for you
since the creation of the world (Matthew 25:34).

Lord, I get excited thinking about the place you've prepared for me when I am taken to heaven to spend eternity with you. But in the meantime, while I'm still here on earth, help me to be faithful in following your commands and in reaching others with your love and provision.

Pinch-hit Mother

⤙⟲⟳⤚

Glenna was getting older, so of course she knew her mother wouldn't be with her much longer. Still, she didn't want to face the reality of losing her until she absolutely had to.

"My husband and I were in Spain, visiting our younger daughter and her family who are missionaries. One morning everyone had gone out to run errands, and I had agreed to stay behind to take care of three-year-old Megan and her baby sister."

The phone rang. Glenna answered it and recognized the voice of her older daughter, Tara. "Brace your heart, Mom," she said, half-sobbing. "Grammy died in her sleep last night."

Taken by surprise, Glenna was clearly shaken. Her mother had not seemed critically ill when she left her just two weeks before. Glenna listened to Tara explain the details. Her mind reeled as she tried to think of what she could do from so far away.

Little Megan was standing near the phone, taking in what she heard. Of course she was concerned when she saw her grandmother burst into tears. At that moment, sweet Megan gently placed her hands in her grandmother's. "Why are you crying, Grammy?" she asked.

Glenna bent down to explain in words she hoped Megan could understand. "Because my mother has just gone to heaven," she said, trying to control her tears.

"Megan looked at me with her soft blue eyes and did her best to console me. 'Don't cry, Grammy,' she said with complete confidence. 'We'll get you another mother.'"

Her concerned smile and tender words turned Glenna's sorrow into laughter.

Reflection

Cast your cares on the LORD and he
will sustain you (Psalm 55:22).

Dear Lord, in times of trial and difficulty the tender words of a young child can be such a healing balm. I am reminded that I must be as a little child myself in order to enter your kingdom when my time on earth is finished.

Dandy Daughters

"Moving my father to an assisted-living facility was one of the most difficult things I've ever done," Annette shared. "I prayed about it for months and consulted friends who had gone this route before me. My three sisters and I had a family meeting and then took turns scouting facilities in our area. We wanted Dad to live within a 20-minute drive of at least one of us."

Finally Annette and her siblings chose Mountain High Assisted Living. It was a beautiful facility situated on a hill overlooking a beautiful town in northern Oregon. "I breathed a sigh of relief the night we moved him in, unpacked his belongings, and got Dad settled into his *new* home after more than 50 years in the house my sisters and I had grown up in."

A week later, after restless nights and a flood of tears, Annette was ready to take him out of the home and move him in with her and her husband, Hunter. "I couldn't stand thinking of Dad declining in this sterile environment surrounded by the wheelchair population." To Annette her father was still youthful and mobile. He just needed extra help.

"Imagine my surprise," she said, "when I went to visit early one morning. There was Dad, the center of attention at the breakfast table, entertaining a host of other men about the same age (80 plus). I listened in on their conversation and soon noticed they were having a ball, regaling one another with stories of their well-lived lives. When one stopped another took over."

When Annette was ready to leave that day, her father whispered in her ear, as he hugged her goodbye, "All of these men came at the urging of their daughters. Isn't that something?" He held Annette by the shoulders and looked her in the eye. "We're all so glad we found each other. Now I have a whole new group of friends."

One of the men, Annette learned, had come up with the phrase "Daughters are dandy." They made a point of repeating the words every time a daughter came to visit and when she was leaving. It became a trademark slogan for this band of cronies!

Annette blew kisses to each one as she sailed out the door. Trailing behind her was a loud chorus of old men chanting, "Daughters are dandy, daughters are dandy, dandy indeed."

Annette smiled all the way home. That night she slept like a daughter should when she knows her father is happy and well-cared for!

Reflection

O Lord, what is man that you care for him, the
son of man that you think of him? (Psalm 144:3).

Oh God, how loving you are to look after my every need from the moment I was born till the moment I pass into eternity. Thank you for guiding my every step, for helping me make wise choices, and then giving me peace of mind even in the midst of bittersweet circumstances.

PART 7

OLD DOG, NEW TRICKS

It All Depends

Phyllis looked at the calendar. January 10. Her sixtieth birthday. Hard to believe she was as old as her grandmother had been when Grammy came to live with Phyllis and her family some 50 years before. Phyllis poked at the gray curls that surrounded her face and tried to smooth the wrinkles that seemed to be multiplying faster than a couple of rabbits.

Phyllis refused to give in to the melancholy mood that was about to overtake her. *I should be giving thanks,* she thought, *instead of grumbling. I've had such a rich and full life. A loving husband, three children, eight grandchildren, dozens of friends, and good health.*

Still Phyllis couldn't shake the reality that she was definitely over the hill and sliding down fast. *In 10 years I'll be 70 and in 10 more, 80.* Now she was really depressed. She *felt* youthful, but she couldn't deny the calendar or the clock. Both were ticking faster than she wanted them to. There was still so much she longed to do with her life. She hadn't written the poetry she dreamed about, and she hadn't yet visited Germany—her parents' native country. And she had always wanted to skydive and go up in a hot air balloon and visit the Holy Land.

Phyllis sat down at her computer and started searching for classes, travel packages, and hot-air balloon rides. She had a lot to accomplish in the next decade, and she wasn't about to wait another moment. While deep in her search, the phone rang. She picked up the receiver and half-listened as she continued clicking the keys. "Phyllis here," she said.

"Hi, Grams. Peter here." Her ten-year-old grandson chuckled as he mimicked her response.

"Why hello, darling," Phyllis cooed. "I love hearing from you."

"Happy birthday," he said and then sang the song to match.

Phyllis got chills listening to him. She could remember when he was a baby and she had rocked and strolled with him day in and day out. What special memories she had.

"Grams, Mom said you're 60 years old today. Is that right?"

"Sure is. I'm getting old on you, aren't I?" she teased.

"I was just wondering…" He paused and cleared his throat. "Does that mean you'll start wearing Pull-Ups?"

Phyllis didn't know whether to laugh or weep. She hadn't thought that far ahead, but apparently Peter had. "So far I'm in good shape," she answered, "but I'll let you know if and when I do, okay?"

"Okay," said Peter. "And Grams, when you do have to wear 'em, I won't tell anyone."

"Glad I can count on you," Phyllis replied.

They said goodbye and hung up. Phyllis picked up the phone again and dialed her travel agent. Her plans were urgent now. She had to get to Israel and Germany, and learn to write poetry, and go up in a hot air balloon, and skydive—all before she reached the age of Pull-Ups.

Reflection

For the LORD is good and his love endures forever;
his faithfulness continues through all generations
(Psalm 100:5).

———————————

Dear Lord, I'm counting on you to sustain me. There is so much I want to do before you call me home to heaven. And while you're at it, please remind me that while I'm walkin' with you there is nothing to fear or fret about.

This Old House

❧

Helen, at age 65, wanted to buy a house of her own. The very idea gave her a nervous twitch and a delightful thrill. She appreciated that her daughter and son-in-law had shared their acreage with her for the past five years. They respected her privacy, and she had no financial worries or concerns about a leaky roof or frozen pipe. But Helen couldn't shake the longing to have a place of her very own, where she could entertain friends, spread out her mementos, plant roses and tulips, and invite out-of-town family to visit.

She toyed with the idea back and forth. One day she was content with what she had, and the next day the longing for her own home returned. She decided to take care of business right then. No more waffling. She'd call a Realtor and start looking.

That action step should help me make a firm decision one way or the other, she mused.

The first day out, the Realtor parked in front of a house with two tall oaks in front and on the side. Rhododendrons edged the foundation and a beautiful maple tree set off the backyard. The house was on a quiet street with a cul-de-sac that opened to miles of swaying grass on the wetlands. And it was just a short walk to the bay that stretched 22 miles across.

Helen stood there imagining her grandchildren and Elizabeth, her Pomeranian, playing in the fenced-in yard and walking with her along the beach. "I tingled just thinking about it," said Helen.

"But then I walked inside and my heart sank. It was a disaster of dark walls, stained and worn carpets, windows broken or missing, and a door hanging by a single hinge. Fortunately the kitchen and breakfast room were a step up, with attractive tile flooring and windows that let in plenty of sunshine."

After looking the place over, Helen and the Realtor parted. They agreed to meet later that day. No matter how many houses Helen drove by, she couldn't get the little one by the bay out of her mind. The next morning she woke up, called the Realtor, and made an offer.

Then came the explaining—to her daughter Kay, to her sister, to her friends, all of whom had a reason why this was the most ridiculous thing she could do at her age.

"Mom," Kay asked, "why do you want to leave us? Who'll help you cut the grass? And what if something breaks?"

Helen stopped, looked her daughter in the eye, and told her the truth about herself at this crucial time in her life. "I've loved living with you and Ron. You've given me so much and I'm grateful. Maybe some day I'll return, if you'll have me, but right now, I'd like to be independent while I'm still able."

Kay looked at her mother. "Okay, Mom. I see what you mean.

You deserve to have your own place. You are always welcome here, and I want to help you in any way I can."

Two months later Helen was in her own house—the one near the bay that simply needed a little fixing up. She had planned to hire a painter and a gardener and a fix-it man, but none of that was necessary. The day after she signed the final documents, her four children, her sisters, her brothers, and all their families converged at the property and began shouting one over the other.

"We're painting the house."

"I'll replace the broken windows."

"I'm repairing the doors."

"I'll take care of the light fixtures."

"I'd like to mow the lawn."

And so it began. Two weeks of painting, hammering, cleaning, mowing, and most of all, laughing. And two weeks of pizza and picnics on the soft green lawn under the shade of the maple tree in Helen's very own yard.

What seemed, at first, like stepping off a cliff, was actually a step into her future.

"I now have a renewed sense of confidence, enthusiasm, and gratitude as I look at the tulips and daffodils blooming everywhere," Helen said. "I love the roses climbing the front fence and the wisteria coming to life in the side yard.

"As the house was transformed, so was I."

Reflection

Your faithfulness continues through all
generations (Psalm 119:90).

Dear Lord, no one can outgive you. Thank you for looking after my most intimate needs, my deepest desires, my heartfelt longings, and then responding with gifts beyond my dreams.

B.A. for M-O-M

⬦

Allison fingered the college applications her twin sons had filled out. They were ready to mail. Her eyes were suddenly misty as she glanced at the family photos lining the staircase of their family home. She remembered her boys when they were little tykes, still holding her hand and sitting on her lap. *Now they're ready to take charge of their own lives. Where have the years gone?* she wondered.

She poured a cup of coffee and sank into the sofa in the family room, awash in memories. She also had some regrets. *I wish I'd gone to college. Dad wanted me to, but I didn't see the point of it at the time. I was focused on getting a job, marrying Emmett, and starting a family.*

Allison picked up the catalog and perused the pages, checking out the courses and the requirements. Her boys had much to be proud of. They more than qualified for university studies. She knew they'd do well in college. They always had been serious about their work. *I wonder how it would have been for me? I was never an honor student—but I never failed anything either.*

The more Allison read, the more interested she became. Her heart fluttered as she imagined herself enrolling in college, walking the campus, attending lectures, serving on committees, planning a future she had never given any thought to before.

Why not? she asked herself. *Who says you have to be 18 to start college or that you have to be 22 when you're finished? Maybe it's the norm, but it's not the only way.*

Allison popped up from the sofa and grabbed the nearest telephone. Charged with adrenaline she punched in the numbers to the admissions office. Before she hung up, she had enrolled in college at age 50. She started with a typing class and a history course. Not too much the first time around.

Today Allison reflects on her first history test. "I was so fearful that I ran to the restroom every few minutes that morning." Just before entering the classroom she made one more stop at the ladies' room, hovering in the stall like a scared rabbit. "I was so nervous I couldn't unlock the door to come out. I didn't want to be late for class, so I crawled out under the door. I remember two girls looking at me like I'd lost it. But I didn't care! I made it to class on time and got an A on the test. Eventually I graduated from junior college with high honors and then received my bachelor's degree with honors at age 55. Getting old is definitely not for wimps. Neither is going to college!" she proclaimed as she pointed to her diploma on the wall in her den.

Reflection

I press on toward the goal to win the prize for
which God has called me heavenward in Christ
Jesus (Philippians 3:14).

Lord, when I set my sights on you and your goal for my life, I am happy and content. What you call me to you equip me for. I never have to worry about not doing the right thing at the right time as long as I listen and follow your perfect plan for me.

Who's on First?

G rams, you have to play. That's what we're here for." Lola looked up from her seat on the bleachers. She had come to the fundraiser to help her grandson Charlie earn money for a trip to a major-league baseball game in Chicago. Fans had paid $10 each to watch a slow-pitch softball game between the junior league players and their grandparents. All proceeds would help pay the team's airfare.

Lola nudged her husband, Russ. "You play, honey. You'll be great—just like you were when we met. Remember?"

Russ rolled his eyes. "No dice, Lola. We both agreed to support Charlie. I wrote the check. You said you'd take a turn at bat. Now keep your promise."

Lola breathed hard and stood up on wobbly legs. She could barely throw a ball, much less hit one. She couldn't see well in the bright sunlight, and if the ball hit her glasses, then what?

She took a deep breath, stepped down from the bench, and took her place in the batter's box.

"Go, Grams, go!" nine-year-old Carla called from her seat.

Lola's daughter Kathy stood up and waved a silk scarf. "You can do it, Mom!"

Lola stepped up to home plate when she heard her name called. The pitcher lobbed the ball. It seemed to be headed straight for her nose. She swayed a bit and then smacked it with all her might. She looked up as the ball arched over second base. She'd done it—a solid hit! The kid guarding the base and those in the field scrambled but no one could catch it. Lola made it to first, and the grandfather ahead of her slid into second. *Safe!*

Lola wiped her forehead and took her position—ready to move when the next batter took his turn. She was darn proud of herself. If only her mother could see her now. Lola had heard over and over that she had no talent for sports. Well, that might have been true at 10, but at 65 she was a star!

Of course it took more than a little getting ready to come this far. That morning she'd spent at least an hour putting herself together. First she cleaned her glasses and put in her removable dental bridge. Next she tied her hair into a ponytail and shoved it into a baseball cap she'd borrowed from Charlie. Then she pulled on her sweatshirt and baggy pants and stepped into a pair of baseball shoes her niece had loaned her. And finally she wrapped her ankle in an Ace bandage, dabbed a bit of makeup on her cheeks, and added blush and lipstick.

If this doesn't beat all. Life is full of surprises. A broken ankle just before Christmas, my sixty-fifth birthday in February, and now charity baseball in May. What's next? I'm afraid to imagine.

The coach called Lola to the batter's box at the bottom of the eighth. *Whack!* She hit another single and made it to first—out of breath when she arrived, but she got there. Surely that counted for something.

It did. Lola went to bat at the top of the ninth too, and she pounded another ball right over the second baseman's head. That drove two team members home and the victory went to the "old" folks, 3 to 2.

"Congratulations!" called the young coach. "How'd you do it? I'm impressed."

Lola adjusted her glasses and pulled the bill on her cap. "Trifocals, a broken ankle, and a removable dental bridge. Works every time! You oughtta try 'em!"

The young man walked away scratching his head but smiling.

Reflection

He gives strength to the weary and increases the
power of the weak (Isaiah 40:29).

———————

Dear God, when I give my all—whether to play a game or complete a task—you're there cheering me on. Thank you for helping me keep on going... even during these golden years.

Turnip Truck

❧⊙❧

Grandpa Harvey had only an eighth-grade education, so when his two grandsons finished high school and began planning for college, he realized they had passed him up. He was often embarrassed when they got into conversations that were over his head, especially when they discovered history. That was one subject he knew little about. When they got to talking about this war and that one, he got so confused he was afraid they might think he was good for nothing but driving a turnip truck. He wasn't ashamed of his farming background, but it was true that he'd spent more time in the fields than he had in a schoolroom.

He recalled a few dates and phrases, such as "Remember the Alamo," although he couldn't recall what it stood for. And he knew that 1620 was the year the Pilgrims landed at Plymouth Rock—or was it? He scratched his head a few times when the boys got into anything he didn't recognize. He wished he'd had the advantages they had. But he didn't, and that was that. He tried to play along and look interested when they shared facts.

One summer he and the boys and their parents took a trip to Washington, D.C.—a first for the entire family. Grandpa Harvey was pretty excited about this adventure. He had always wanted to see the White House, the Washington Monument, and the Lincoln Memorial. And he'd heard about the Smithsonian Natural History Museum.

"This'll be my chance to brush up," he told Jeb and Kurt. "Maybe I'll catch up to you two history wizards," he joked.

"Way to go, Grandpa," said Kurt. "We'll all learn something, I'm sure."

On the third day of their week, the family set out for the Smithsonian. They moved from one exhibit to another, stopping here and there to chat about what they saw and discussing what they'd do next.

Jeb tapped his grandfather on the shoulder. "I'm really interested in finding the section with Greek and Roman artifacts," he said. "How about you?"

Grandpa didn't know anything about either one, but it sounded fine to him. "Sure!" he said. "Let's go." He was ready to learn something new. Everyone agreed they'd go together. They stopped at an intersection to read the signs so they'd head in the right direction. They had three choices.

Grandpa Harvey wanted to help in the decision-making, so he turned to the family and grinned with confidence. He remembered something he had learned years ago. Now was the time to show 'em what he knew. "Appears to me you can take any one of the three," he said with a glint in his eye. "Don't all roads lead to Rome?"

Jeb and Kurt burst out laughing.

"Hey, Grandpa, you know more than we thought you did!" Grandpa winked and led the family down the right road—straight to the Roman history exhibit!

Reflection

As the Scripture says, "Anyone who trusts in him will never be put to shame" (Romans 10:11).

Lord, how easy it is to be embarrassed by my lack, whatever it might be: education, money, prestige, intelligence, appearance. But you don't measure me by any of these. You delight in me just as I am because you created me for your pleasure. Let me put my trust in you alone and hold my head high as we walk together.

Nothin' to Stew About

Rose could hardly wait to board the train from Kalamazoo, Michigan, to Chicago, Illinois. She was one of ten men and women from her church invited to participate in an outreach to inner-city families. Her duties included cooking, facilitating a Bible study for the women and men, playing with the children, and caring for the elderly.

Rose was no youngster herself, but she was still strong and able-bodied. She had plenty of life experiences to share with these weary families who had so little—some not even enough food to keep body and soul together.

The first evening there, Rose volunteered to lead worship and to set up a room for the Bible study. She was comfortable in front of a group, and she was especially excited about bringing the Word of God to these people. Just as she was about to test the microphone and put the last few chairs in place, one of the ministers from the host church came up to her. "I heard you make a mean beef stew," he said. "I'd like you to take over in the kitchen. Things

193

are pretty rowdy back there. One of the deacons mentioned you can pull a meal together in minutes—even for a big crowd."

"But I'm in the middle of..." She pointed to the room set-up.

"No problem," he said. "We'll get one of the men to finish the job." The minister walked away.

Rose was insulted. *Just like a man*, she thought. *Stick the women in the kitchen and put the men up front.* "God, this is not fair!" she moaned. She had her heart set on sharing Jesus with the crowd, not being stuck in front of an old stove in an ancient kitchen. But she didn't have a choice. The minister had practically ordered her to cook the meal. She made her way to the kitchen. She peeled the carrots, chopped up the stew meat, cut the potatoes—grumbling with every stroke of the knife.

Then an amazing thing happened. Mothers and fathers and toddlers and teens and boys and girls in-between were walking hand-in-hand in front of the kitchen window on their way to the meeting hall. The setting sun glistened in the background and soft music began to play from the overhead speaker. "Jesus loves me, this I know..."

Rose stopped for a moment, looked out, and listened. *What a scene! People walking and talking together on their way to hear the Word of God. What we came for is already taking place.*

The team was serving these people by their very presence. The families were excited judging from the lilt in their voices and the quickness of their steps.

"To think that just a few moments ago I was caught up in my own delusion of what my mission should be," Rose mused. "I wanted to serve God and these people in *my* way, not God's."

Rose turned back to the stove and the huge cauldron of stew

on the back burner. She pulled it to the front, added more carrots, potatoes, and a can of corn. *Imagine this! I get to be the "chef for the day" in the Lord's kitchen. What an honor!*

Rose dipped a ladle into the pot and brought up enough stew to taste. Hands down, it was the best stew she'd ever made!

Reflection

The kingdom of God is not a matter of eating and drinking, but of righteousness, peace and joy in the Holy Spirit (Romans 14:17).

Lord, thank you for showing me that my agenda has more to do with pleasing and serving myself than doing what will bless and encourage your people. Help me mend my selfish ways and lean on You for direction.

Flower Power

❧

'm tired of planting flowers that die or succumb to bugs," Les told his wife, Minnie. He shook his head and let out a deep breath. "What do you say we pick out some fake bloomers, and we'll have color all year long without the fuss and financial drain?"

Minnie had wanted pots of living marigolds and geraniums, but she too was ready to call it quits. The couple had spent a lot of money on blooming plants year after year, but they simply didn't last. The next day they headed for Michaels, "The Arts and Crafts Store," and in a few minutes they found four beautiful faux bushes. And they were on sale! The two were thrilled. "We knew this was the answer to our gardening dilemma," asserted Les.

They also purchased a spray bottle of artificial flower cleaner. All they had to do was spritz the blooms and leaves whenever they got dusty, and they'd be as beautiful as ever as soon as they dried. What could be easier? This was their kind of gardening.

Les and Minnie were both happy with this set-up for well over a year. Then one day everything changed. While eating breakfast one morning Minnie looked outside, caught by the strands of blue and gold and orange that broke across the sky as the sun popped up.

"I watched the sunrise in awe," she said, "and then lowered my eyes to avoid the glare. That's when I saw *it*. The tiny head of a marigold pushing its way up from the soil leftover in the pots on our front deck. Attached were several buds about to break into full bloom. I chuckled out loud. *Go, Mari, go!* I thought. It was fighting for its space even though the faux bush took up most of the room.

"Les," she squeaked, "look at this! The marigolds are back, and they appear to be thriving." Minnie couldn't imagine how. She hadn't watered or fertilized or given any thought to them since she threw the last of the bunch out and replaced them with the fake bouquets.

Grace, she thought. *It's God's grace. How else could they survive?*

As Minnie looked closer, the contrast between the genuine and the counterfeit startled her. "The real flower was full of life and power and grit. I could feel it as well as see it," Minnie related. "The imposter was a cheap imitation I had grown bored with because there was no growth and no surprises."

Gosh, Lord, are You trying to tell me something here?

The faux flowers of life are often such a good imitation of the real that we can't tell them apart—until God disturbs the under-soil of our lives and pushes through with grace and guidance, causing us to bloom where we're planted.

Reflection

It will burst into bloom; it will rejoice greatly
and shout for joy (Isaiah 35:2).

Lord, thank You for showing me an important life lesson. To serve You requires that I be real, keep growing even when it's tough, and hold up my head as I push through the hardships of life. Walkin' with You certainly is not for wimps!

Dig In

Jesse felt as though he couldn't win for losing. His wife, Martha, wanted him to help out with the cooking and chores now that he was retired from his printing shop. But he didn't know the first thing about dusting and vacuuming or putting a meal on the table. She had taken care of all that for 45 years.

"You can't teach an old dog new tricks," he said whenever she brought up the subject.

"It's not a trick," she retorted. "It's common sense. You take a cloth and run it over the furniture. You turn on the vacuum and run that over the carpet. And as for cooking, I'd welcome even a bowl of soup or oatmeal, a slice of toast with butter and jam, a hot dog, a baked potato, a cookie, tea, a hard-boiled egg, that sort of thing," she said motioning to the pantry and fridge. "Nothing fancy; just a break from the routine. You could make any one of those items. You don't need a cookbook."

With that Martha headed out the door, calling over her

shoulder that she was off to the hairdresser's and would be back in time for dinner—about 6:00. "See you then," she said and blew Jesse a kiss.

He sat down at the kitchen table and mulled over what his wife had said. It sunk in. She deserved some time off from domestic duties. If he could retire, why couldn't she—at least part-time?

He knew just what to do. He'd fix dinner and surprise her when she returned home.

He knew a few things after watching her all these years. He tossed up a quick prayer, turned on the oven, pulled out a few pots and pans, rolled up his sleeves, and got to work.

By 5:45 the entire meal was ready. He couldn't wait for Martha to walk through the door. At 6:00 on the dot she sailed in, looking as pretty as a picture in her new hairdo. His heart skipped a beat. She had a few wrinkles and her hair had turned white, as had his, but darned if she wasn't the same lovely girl he'd married all those years ago.

"Welcome home, honey," he cooed. "Dinner's ready!"

Martha beamed. "You ordered take-out?" she asked. "How nice."

"No! I cooked the meal myself. Pull up a chair, and I'll serve you."

Martha spread the napkin in her lap and waited as Jesse laid out the very meal she had requested: a bowl of soup, a bowl of oatmeal, a slice of toast with butter and jam, a hot dog, a baked potato, a cookie, tea, and a hard-boiled egg.

Jesse stood by waiting for her response. Martha looked a bit puzzled at first, but then her mouth curled into a smile. She stood up and hugged him. "I've been thinking about a meal like this all day," she declared.

Reflection

Come to me, all you who are weary and burdened, and I will give you rest (Matthew 11:28).

———————

Dear Lord, thank you for providing in the most amazing and unexpected ways!

Walkin' to Win

The year I turned 50 I did something remarkable—remarkable for me, that is. I signed up for an all-women's beginner's backpack trip in Yosemite National Park. Hiking to the top of the famous Half Dome had been a dream of mine for many years, so when the opportunity came up, I went for it. I spent months getting in shape with weekly workouts. I learned all I could about tents, boots, backpacks, and dehydrated food.

When I returned home, I was eight pounds lighter and felt ten years younger. I committed then to do at least one thing each year that would stretch me in an exciting way. Today I look back over a myriad of activities that have expanded my life in ways I never could have imagined—from teaching myself to sketch to taking a ropes course with my grandson.

I remember the day of the ropes course well. The moment I reached out from the safety of the climbing pole to the ropes that stretched before me, my legs shook, my heart raced, and my palms broke out in perspiration. *What is going on with you, girl?* I chided myself. *You're a 60-year-old woman. Get a grip.* "On a rocking chair, maybe," I muttered.

I like excitement, some risk, and lots of adventure. And it had better be fun or I won't do it again. Well, rope climbing was a lot of things but *fun* wasn't one of them. However, that summer I had gotten myself into this by telling my grandson and his dad that I'd join them, so I was determined to stick it out.

By the time I returned to the starting point, my hands were red and raw from rope burns and my knees were sore from knocking. But I made it to the finish! I shinnied down the pole feeling groovy, feeling alive, feeling set free of the thoughts that wanted to hold me back.

It was a lot like walkin' with God. I don't always know the way or how it's going to work out, but I know the God I'm walkin' with and that's enough for me. It's always exciting, risky, adventuresome, and fun. It's life in abundance—just as Jesus promised.

Reflection

For whoever finds me finds life and receives
favor from the LORD (Proverbs 8:35).

———————

Lord, may I never stop short of going all the way with you, wherever you lead and regardless of the circumstances. I want to experience all that you've planned for me.

Slow Down

Try this. Place your hands—palms up—in your lap. Examine them carefully. Do you have time on your hands? Probably not. At least not if your job involves sitting at a computer, loading a truck, teaching kindergarten, changing a hospital bed, rustling up a meal for the next customer, editing a manuscript, presiding over a board meeting, driving a taxi, directing a play, writing a magazine article, trying a lawsuit, balancing a company's books...or any number of other work-related tasks.

"If only I did have a bit of time on my hands," you might be saying. "Oh, what I would do with even five or ten extra minutes. Take a hot bath, paint my toenails, build a birdhouse, mow the lawn, mulch my flowerbed, steep a tea bag in boiling water, say a prayer, sit and do nothing! Now *there's* a thought."

Time—if only there were more of it. Or more energy to accomplish your goals in the time you do have. But wait! Do you want to keep falling prey to the tyranny of time? Our culture is inundated with time management tools: date books, pocket calendars, wristwatches with built-in alarms, beepers for belt, briefcase, or handbag, bestselling books, computer programs, and seminars on how to save, spend, invest, maximize, and catch time before it flies away.

What if time were not the fleeting, tyrannizing resource we are taught to believe it is? What if we chose instead to view time as an expression of God? As part of His very nature and plan. Would we so anxiously live by deadlines, join the morning rat race, or grab a minute and run with it? Wouldn't we, instead, be moved to rethink and perhaps reshape the way we use time? Perhaps our goal would be stewardship rather than management. As stewards we might be more open to the purposes set down by the Chief Steward. Rather than accomplishing and accumulating according to some deadline, we might share our time by serving others—as well as serving ourselves—in Jesus' name.

When we look at time in this way there really is plenty to go around—for others and for ourselves. There is time for everything under the sun if we take a moment to notice and then give ourselves to that season. Time to plant, to harvest, to find, to lose, to tear, to repair, to be quiet, to speak up, to wage war, to experience peace—there is time. And there is time enough to create a work of art, to read a book, to say a prayer, to be alone, to be with others, to grow roses—and to notice God in all of it.

There is a right time for everything.

Reflection

There is a time for everything, and a season for
every activity under heaven (Ecclesiastes 3:1).

206 • Gettin' Old Ain't for Wimps Volume 2

Lord God, help me be a good steward of the time you've given me, whether I'm changing a tire or changing a diaper, making cookies or making a speech, standing in line or standing in worship. May every moment of my life be lived for your glory.

PART 8

BODY WORKS

Fall on Your Knees

Garth walked forward at church on Christmas morning after an inspiring service and received Jesus Christ as his personal Savior. His wife, Jeanette, stayed in the pew, blotting the tears that poured down her cheeks. For 40 years she'd been praying for this moment.

"Oh God, how thankful I am for your mercy and goodness," she prayed as she watched her precious husband make a commitment of faith. Their life together was about to be transformed. She knew it.

Garth returned to the seat next to her and squeezed her hand. His eyes shone and there was a softness around his mouth and chin that had not been there before. She shivered at the sight of this changed man she had shared her life with for so long.

Afterward, in the lobby, longtime friends came forward to congratulate and bless Garth on this important step. He had often accompanied Jeanette to church but had never participated in any of the songs or rituals.

The couple decided to continue their celebration over lunch

at Dan's Deli. As they sat in their favorite corner booth, Garth seemed preoccupied and almost sullen. Jeanette feared something was terribly wrong.

She reached across the table and took his hand. "What is it?" she asked.

"I'm worried about something."

"Want to talk about it?" Jeanette felt her heart pound a bit too fast.

"Seems like Christians sing and talk a lot about falling on their knees. It was in one of the Christmas carols this morning, and the elder who prayed with me suggested I kneel so he could lay hands on my head."

"Why is that a problem?" Jeanette asked, curious about this concern.

"With these bum knees," he said, "I'm afraid I'll fall down all right and won't be able to get up."

Jeanette stifled a laugh. "God will understand," she said. "You get a break until after you have your knee replacement surgery next month."

Reflection

Your words have supported those who stumbled;
you have strengthened faltering knees (Job 4:4).

Dear God, You're a God of mercy and kindness. You never expect from me more than I can give or handle. When I think I can't go on, you provide the grace I need to keep going with you.

Frazzled

arriet had let herself go—go to the ice cream shop, the bagel shop, and the candy shop. She knew she was eating too much junk. She felt achy all over—head, stomach, back, arms, and legs. She was a mess and she knew it. Every time she thought about exercising she became frantic and frazzled. Just the thought of driving to a gym, changing clothes, pumping iron, and getting sweaty was enough to set her teeth on edge. Still she knew she had to do something.

One morning while running errands in the neighborhood shopping center, she noticed a sign in the window of an exercise studio: "Senior aerobics here." That sounded like fun. And she liked the fact that the focus was men and women over 60.

She asked her doctor's permission because she didn't want to do anything that would overtax her heart. "Go for it. It'll do you good," Dr. Barnes said when she phoned his office. So she went for it. She bought herself a leotard, tights, and a new towel for drying off when the class was over.

The first session turned out to be quite a workout. She stooped and stood, turned and twisted, pushed and pulled, jumped up and down, and broke a sweat for more than an hour. By the time she got the leotard and tights on, the class was over.

Reflection

Now that you know these things, you will be blessed if you do them (John 13:17).

———————

Lord, I know I should take care of my body and soul, my mind and my heart. But I so often wait too long and then, when I take action, it takes me so long to get it together that I miss the blessing completely. Please help me today to walk with you and not drag behind where I so easily lose sight of the goal you have for me.

Hair Ye! Hair Ye!

✿❮❪✿

Jane looked in the mirror at her straggly hair. "What am I going to do with you? I'm getting fat, and you're getting thin. It's not fair!"

She raked her fingers through the gray strands, remembering how her late husband, Terry, had loved her hair when they first met. It was golden then—and thick. Now at age 60, it needed all the help she could give it—perms, thickeners, a weekly shampoo and styling. But nothing gave it the look she wanted. When it came right down to it, she was losing her hair and there was no getting it back.

Jane dressed for the day, and then checked the mailbox. The carrier usually arrived around nine o'clock each morning. She pulled out a handful of envelopes and leafed through them. Bills, flyers, ads. *Nothing exciting here.*

Then a catalog caught her attention. The model on the front smiled from the page. *Her* hair was gorgeous, thick, flowing, wavy—just what Jane wanted. The headline beneath the picture beckoned: "WIG ISSUE—SEE INSIDE FOR BEAUTIFUL, NATURAL HAIRPIECES."

Just what Jane used to have and was now desperate for. She tore through the pages, her hands shaking. Could this be the answer to her problem? A wig. *Why didn't I think of it before? Thank you, Lord. You always provide.*

Jane grabbed her credit card, dialed the 800 number, and talked to a representative about the perfect wig for her. After their consultation, Jane made her choice and placed the order. She hung up and looked at herself in the hall mirror. *I'm on the way to being a new woman. No more plain Jane!*

She kept her purchase a secret from her daughter, Kim, who lived with her, and from her best friend, Dotty, who lived across the street.

The wig arrived on Saturday while Kim was on duty at the hospital. Jane tore open the package and pulled the hairpiece over her head. *Gorgeous!* She couldn't help but touch the soft curls and run her hand through the gentle waves. She loved the sheen and the texture and the way it felt. In fact, she was sure she stood taller and looked much prettier than she had in years.

She decided to debut her new wig the following day. On Sunday morning she walked into the kitchen. Kim looked surprised and then delighted.

"Mom, you look *fab!* A wig, I presume."

"Ah," Jane mumbled, "I hoped it wouldn't be *that* obvious."

"Mom, get real. You've hated your hair for years."

Jane shrugged, grabbed her purse and keys, and headed for the car.

She drove to church in silence, but she noticed Kim looking her over and smiling.

What a morning. By the time they returned home Jane was flying. Angie had said she looked great. Barbara said she nearly didn't recognize her. And Dotty stood back and yelped, "Jane, it's a new you. I love it!"

By mid-week, Jane was so attached to her wig, she wore it from the moment she woke up till she went to sleep. It needed a small size adjustment, but she didn't want to part with it long enough to send it back.

The following Friday morning, Jane stopped at a coffee shop while doing errands. She ordered a cup of mocha and a muffin, and then sat down to read the paper and relax. It was a warm day, and the steaming beverage made her hot! She fanned her face with the menu and felt trickles of perspiration run down her face. She ran her hands through her hair to cool off.

Suddenly she realized something was wrong! She reached up. The wig was gone. She panicked.

"Looking for this?" a gentleman asked, stifling a laugh.

"Yes, and thanks," she mumbled.

Jane grabbed the mass of moist curls and ran out of the shop mortified. She prayed no one she knew had seen her.

How humiliating, Lord. How can I wear this thing? It can't be trusted!

At the car Jane took a deep breath, pulled on the wig, and checked herself in the car mirror. Then she got the giggles. Soon she was laughing so hard she was shaking. "God, is this funny or what? I'm remembering the scripture that tells me that you know the number of hairs on my head. Do the ones on my wig count too?"

Reflection

Indeed, the very hairs of your head
are all numbered (Luke 12:7).

Thank you, Lord, that I can cry with you…and laugh, as well. You are so good to me, caring for my every move, my every desire, my every fear, my every insecurity. I am so glad you are my Father, my protector, my provider. Because of you, I can find hope and humor in everything that occurs.

Front and Center

⌒◯⌒◯⌒

Mary, the church organist, called early one Sunday morning as Ruth and her husband were preparing to leave for the first service. "Ruth, can you cover for me? I'm feeling ill."

Ruth was happy to help out, even though it meant rushing around at the last moment putting music together.

It was a hot and humid day so this added to the last-minute stress. The temperature had already reached 92 degrees at eight o'clock. "I knew I'd be sitting on a keyboard bench for over an hour," said Ruth. "The thought of wearing panty hose was unbearable.

"Then I remembered my sister had given me a can of Air Stocking to spray on my legs when I want to appear that I'm wearing hose or sporting a great tan. It also helps cover my veins."

Ruth rushed out to their sun deck and sprayed both legs up and down. She loved the idea of looking good and being cool at the same time.

On to church! She and her husband arrived minutes before the service began. Ruth jumped out of the car and raced ahead of John so she could get situated at the organ. Suddenly, she felt her husband's hand on her shoulder.

"John pulled me aside and chuckled. 'Ruth, I thought you used the spray on your legs?'"

"Of course I did. Look for yourself." Ruth felt indignant that he'd question her now, when she was in a hurry. "I glanced at the front of my legs, and they looked fine to me," said Ruth.

"Check the backs and just below your knees," John persisted, pointing and laughing. "I can see the line on each side where you stopped!"

By this time he was laughing so hard he had tears in his eyes. Ruth admitted she was mortified. "My skirt wasn't a mini by any means, but it wasn't long enough to cover my mistake either. By then there was no time to return home and undo the damage. It was one day when I hoped no one would pay any attention to me!"

Ruth remembered a passage in scripture that reminds us not to ask the Lord to guide our footsteps unless we are willing to move our feet.

"That morning," she said, "I moved my feet all right, nearly running to the front of the church."

Thankfully, no one said a thing to Ruth about her "interesting" leg wear. Her husband, well he's another matter.

"He continues to tease me about my one-sided hose!" Ruth says with a laugh.

Reflection

[He] gives grace to the humble (Proverbs 3:34).

———————

Dear Lord, how embarrassing are those moments when I am suddenly exposed—whether physically or emotionally. I want to crawl in a hole or bury my head under the covers rather than face someone's judgment or ridicule or laughter. But then I think about the way you were humiliated and mortified on earth. You always remained humble and contrite. Thank you for your example.

The Other Shirl

S hirl and her husband, Mel, raced around the house at the last moment. They had ordered movie tickets online for themselves and their friends Jim and his wife, referred to as "the *other* Shirl."

"I laid the receipt on the coffee table in the den," Shirl called from the bedroom, where she was touching up her lipstick and looking for her pink sweater.

"Not here," Mel called back.

"Where could it be? I put it there myself." Shirl ran into the den and there on the coffee table was the receipt.

"Here it is. How could you have missed it?" Shirl let out a long breath, tucked the paper into her purse, and headed for the front door. "Mel, we'll be late if we don't get into the car this minute. What's going on?"

"Can't find my glasses," Mel shouted from the living room. "I was sure I left them on the end table after reading the newspaper."

Shirl let out another long breath. *Well, that explains why he couldn't find the movie tickets receipt.*

"I knew you should have ordered a spare pair…too late now. Let's go. I'll fill you in on the plot if you can't see well enough."

"I'll get by," Mel muttered and off they went.

They picked up "the other Shirl" and her husband, Jim. While waiting in line at the theater, Jim started fiddling with his hearing aid. It squawked and squeaked as he tried to adjust it to the right volume. Then he realized the batteries were low. "I guess I'll have to make do without them," he told the others.

The women looked at each other and rolled their eyes. Mel's Shirl had told Jim's Shirl about Mel's misplaced glasses and now Jim's Shirl would have a "husband story" of her own. After the movie the couples stopped at Reggie's Deli for a cold drink and a sandwich. As they were about to eat, "the other Shirl" leaned in and said in a loud voice, "Okay, Mel…you tell Jim what you *heard*…and Jim, you tell Mel what you *saw!*"

The four cracked up laughing. Shirl and "the other Shirl" gave each other a high five.

Reflection

Forget the former things; do not dwell
on the past (Isaiah 43:18).

Lord, the changes I face are annoying and sometimes embarrassing, but you encourage me to keep going forward and to let go of the things of the past. Even though my hearing and my eyesight are not what they once were, it doesn't matter when it comes to my relationship with you. You have given me eyes to see and ears to hear your Word.

Seeing Is Believing

Virginia was diagnosed with macular degeneration. What a blow! It made a huge impact on her life. She could no longer enjoy the many things she had taken for granted for so long, such as reading and even watching movies and television. She had to get a special monitor for her computer, and she could no longer drive.

Everything she wanted to do had to be considered in a new way due to the change in her eyesight. Art and knitting and card playing were now a struggle, whereas a decade before they were a part of her regular routine.

Virginia received treatment for two years. During one of her checkups she felt hopeful for the first time in months. "I was overjoyed that I could read the big 'E' on the eye chart. During previous appointments I wasn't able to read any of the letters," she said.

Virginia couldn't help but blurt out her excitement over her progress. "Now may I have my driver's license back?"

The assistant winked. "When you get on the road," she quipped, "call and let us know, so we can get off!"

Reflection

And I—in righteousness I will see your face;
when I awake, I will be satisfied with seeing
your likeness (Psalm 17:15).

Dear Lord, the prospect of failing eyesight is frightening to think about and even more scary to endure. But I have your promise that you will always be with me, so I trust that even if my eyes fail me, you never will. You will guide me all the days of my life on earth and forever after.

What?

Sally and Debra, ages 53 and 57 respectively, bought an aerobics studio. They'd been looking for something to do now that their children were grown and the grandkids were in junior high. It was about time they started taking up their own lives. The women wanted to feel useful again, to be needed, and to get back in shape. It simply wasn't okay with Sally to have to suck in her belly every time she zipped her jeans. And Debra was determined to give up her hobby—baking pies from scratch. Tart boysenberry with real whipped cream and a sprinkle of cinnamon and caramel-covered pecans was her downfall. She'd pulled Sally into the pie abyss with her, and the two decided they had to do something. Stretching and bending and sliding across the floor to loud music seemed just right. And they'd be doing it with other women—their new clients—so there'd be no going back to their old habits. Then maybe they could afford a slice of pie or two once in a great while, and it wouldn't make that much of a difference on their figures.

After the first year in business, they both looked at each other. Did they want to continue teaching aerobics? Were they achieving their goals? They decided they were, sort of. Sally could zip up her jeans more easily now, and Debra had definitely cut back on pie baking. But were they fulfilled? Was it enough to bounce across the floor, squat, bend, lunge, and do the grapevine day after day? Was there more to life?

"I know," Sally offered one day as she bounded up the steps to the aerobic center, "let's donate blood. The Red Cross has announced a critical need for blood donors. We could go down to the blood bank after class."

"Good idea," Debra agreed. "I've never done that before. It's time I offered."

Later that day the two women drove to the blood bank and were impressed at how many people in their age range were there to donate. They were feeling quite noble as they joined the line of other gray heads. After a preliminary check-in and check-up, they were both turned down! Sally learned that her blood pressure was too high. She'd need to visit a physician first—to see if she had high blood pressure, which might require medication to manage it. Until it was under control, she couldn't be a donor. Debra was even more surprised to be turned down. She'd gotten a tiny butterfly tattoo on her right arm two weeks before "just for fun," as she put it. She discovered that day that anyone with a tattoo cannot donate blood for one year after the procedure.

The women left the blood bank feeling discouraged and rejected—even if for good causes. Debra took a deep breath and held her head high. "There's only one thing to do when you're pushing 60, forgetting things you used to recall easily, and getting turned down by the American Red Cross."

"What's that?" Sally asked, eager to find out the secret.

"Eat pie!" Debra exclaimed and then giggled like a high school girl. "And I know just where to get two slices of boysenberry with real whipped cream and a sprinkle of cinnamon and caramel-covered pecans."

Sally licked her lips and smiled. "I bet you do. Come on, sister, lead the way!"

Reflection

Humble yourselves, therefore, under God's mighty hand, that he may lift you up in due time (1 Peter 5:6).

———————

Lord, thank you that I can laugh at myself when things don't go the way I want them to…or as I expect them to. The important thing is my attitude. May I always hold the light of your love in my thoughts, words, and deeds.

Just Desserts

❦

Ninety-year-old Marvin loved sweets—no getting around that. Chocolate mousse, caramel pecan turtle cheesecake, apple streusel, triple berry cream pie, and any kind of candy or ice cream. The list was endless. "If it's sweet, it's neat!" according to Marvin.

Marvin's doctor didn't share his patient's passion. He was more concerned with Marvin's general health—and his heart and cholesterol, in particular. During his last checkup Marvin half-listened to Dr. Brown's suggestions about curbing the sweets, substituting the high-calorie and high-fat desserts for low-cal, no-fat gelatin treats, or, better yet, fresh fruit.

"Doc, lo-cal, no-fat, no fun, no thanks!"

"Marvin, my job is to help you live a long and healthy life."

"Doc, congratulations. You've achieved your goal," Marvin replied. "I'm 90!" With that Marvin walked out of the office and met his friend Harry for a triple latte with real whipped cream and a slice of double-chocolate fudge at Minerva's Bakery.

Marvin enjoyed telling Harry about the conversation in his physician's office. Harry brightened and leaned forward. Marvin could tell he was about to be lectured. It was something Harry loved to do—tell other people how to live their lives—though he rarely told himself the same thing.

"Marvin, I really think you should give more thought to Dr. Brown's advice. He's been looking out for you for the last 30 years. You owe him that much, don't you think?" Harry sat back and crossed his arms. "I'll support you. We'll give up these decadent desserts and go on a fresh fruit binge. It's summer so it'll be easy with all the berries and melons in season. What do you say? Is it a deal?"

Marvin slammed his fist on the table. His coffee cup jumped. "No deal!" he declared. "Why should I change what's working for me? I love sweets. Enough said. When in doubt, don't change desserts, change doctors."

Reflection

Teach the older men to be temperate…self-controlled, and sound (Titus 2:2).

———

Lord, it's tough to be disciplined. I linger over the dessert tray, loiter at the ice cream counter, pace back and forth in the bakery. I'm always tempted to eat what looks and tastes good. Help me enjoy the natural, good foods you have provided and focus on living, not eating.

Seeing Your Smile

Ⓞⓝⓞ

On Monday morning Tonia looked in the mirror. *Oy!* She let out a deep sigh. The wrinkles were taking over her face faster than the snails were ravaging her flower garden. She had to do something and do it quick. She was nearly 70, and time was running out. Pretty soon there wouldn't be enough smooth skin left to push, pull, prod, or pin up!

She sat down at her laptop and spent an hour looking at the many ways she could improve her appearance and lop off a decade or so. There was the usual surgical facelift. And there was non-surgical microdermabrasion, a peeling of the outer layer of skin, resulting in a smoother, younger look.

She'd also heard about acupuncture treatments for the face. She didn't know much about that procedure but the thought of a bunch of needles poking out of her cheeks and forehead didn't sound appealing.

What to do? Tonia hoped she'd find just the right procedure for her and the money to carry it out. She decided to pray and wait—and see what answer God would bring.

That afternoon she ran a few errands—dropped off clothes at the cleaners, picked up a few groceries, paid her phone and utility bills. While walking to her car in front of Top Hill Market, Tonia spotted Angie Cranwell, her neighbor's grown daughter.

"Tonia, hi," shouted Angie as she ran up beside her. "How are you? It's been such a long time since we've seen each other. You look wonderful."

Tonia hugged Angie and asked a few questions about the young woman's family, work, and her new home.

Angie was quick to share details. Then she glanced at her watch. "Oops. Gotta run. Have to pick up Robbie from preschool and then meet a painter. We're having the entire house brightened up a bit."

Tonia squeezed Angie's hand and kissed her cheek. "I'll have to stop by when you're finished. I'd love to see what you've done."

Angie smiled. "Absolutely." Then she paused for a moment and leaned in. "Tonia, I must say you look beautiful. I hope I'm half as attractive as you are when I'm your age. Just seeing your smile gives me a lift." With that she turned and dashed to her car.

Tonia stood in the middle of the driveway stunned. *Did I hear Angie correctly? That my smile gave her a lift? What an unexpected compliment!*

Tonia drove home, plopped the groceries onto the kitchen table, and ran into her bedroom. She stood in front of the full-length mirror and surveyed her face once again. She liked what she saw: bright blue eyes that sparkled, even white teeth, a pleasing hairdo with soft, blond highlights, and a smile that had lifted a friend's day.

"Thank you, God," she murmured. "I get it. The best face-lift—and the most affordable—is a smile."

Reflection

The king is enthralled by your beauty; honor him, for he is your lord (Psalm 45:11).

———————

Dear God, I lift my face in praise to you this day.

Not My Club

⤜⟶⟵⤛

One thing for sure, Patsy was not going to be one of those old ladies with gray corkscrew curls all over her head, plump arms that jiggled when she reached for a glass of water, and a belly that spilled over her waistline—or what was left of it. She couldn't stop the aging process, but she could control how she looked while going through it. She kept her weight in line, walked for an hour every day, attended a dance workout two days a week, and on a very good day she wasn't above climbing part way up a tree with her five-year-old grandson. No senior club for Patsy. She was going to be "forever young"…at least in her mind.

Patsy lived her life with this attitude and commitment. She carried it with her when she and her husband signed up for a cruise in the Bahamas one week in July. She bought a new batch of summer clothes, including cut-offs, flip-flops, a big straw hat with a blue-and-white ribbon, and a jeans jacket with the words MAJOR BABE embroidered on the back. A daring move, but one she enjoyed. If people looked her way in dismay, well, at least they looked. That couldn't be all bad, could it?

At 72 she was a major babe in every way—at least to her way of thinking. She still sang solos in the church choir, headed up a committee on civic fiscal responsibility in her community, and taught a Bible study to a group of 30-something women. She was also a respected member of a group of retired businesswomen.

The day she and Herb boarded the ship, however, she thought she'd crumble. It seemed everywhere she looked there were gray heads—and many of the women had the corkscrew curls she detested—some gray and some blond and some brown—as if they were trying to fool someone. What club was this, anyway?

She and Herb were planning to cut a rug when the music came on that night. They always cleared the floor when they danced, and she was determined to walk the deck every day to keep her figure in check. Four laps equaled a mile. So 12 laps would give her three miles—taking up an hour—the amount of time she walked at home.

The first night in their cabin Patsy poured out her concern to Herb. "I think I made a big mistake. We're with a bunch of old people, and I don't like it. I was hoping there'd be some people like us. All I'm seeing are crow's feet, turkey necks, bald spots, gray curls, and floppy arms. We're in the wrong club."

Herb sidled up to Patsy and put his arm around her shoulder. He steered her to the closest mirror. "Take a good hard look at us, sweetheart. This *is* our club."

Patsy let out a long sigh and then a hearty chuckle. Herb was right. He had a turkey neck. She had crow's feet, and the flesh on her arms—though slender—jiggled at least a little when she reached for a bath towel. And her hair, wavy and attractively cut, was gray going on snow-white.

They dressed, walked to the dining room, and sat at a table of people new to them—yet familiar at the same time. They were all in this together—upstanding members of the Golden Years Club.

Reflection

They will still bear fruit in old age; they will stay
fresh and green (Psalm 92:14).

Lord, this is my club. I'm a senior now, and I need to give myself to where I am, not where I wish I were.

Acknowledgments

I wish to thank these men and women for contributing their ideas, experiences, and story seeds—all of which have been woven into the fabric of my writing.

Charlotte Adelsperger • Bev Adler • Nicole Amsler • Barbara Anson • Marie Asner • Amy C. Baker • Millie Barger • Ralph Bender • Betty Blyler • Nargis Bunce • Janet Burr • Michele Buschman • Amy Canada • Shirley Carson • Marge Carter • Glenna Clark • Joan Clayton • Dale and Dolores Collins • Eleanor Cowles • Dean Crowe • Mona Downey • Sharon Norris Elliott • Lorraine Espinosa • Pat Evans • Sylvia Everett • Pam Farrell • Lana Fletcher • Marilou Flinkman • Charles Flowers • Annette Freligh • Freda Fullerton • Vernette Fulop • Joyce A. Gendusa • Dianne Geisler • Millie Gess • Kathleen Gibson • Judy Gilboe • Alice King Greenwood • Peggy Hamburg • Jeanette Hanscome • Margo Haren • Joann Hawkins • John and Edie Holm • Marsha Hubler • Angela Hunt • Loralee Hunt • Shelley Hussey • Patti Iverson • Linda Jewell • Veda Boyd Jones • Susan Keck • Mary Kirk • James Lamb • Judith Larmon • Shirley Longlois • Patricia Lorenz • Brad McBrayer • Mary McCormick • Jim McEldowney • Brenda McKee • Joan McMahon • Louisa Godissart McQuillen • Karen Milam • Sharon Moore • Sherrie Murphree • Irma Newland • Penny Pfister Newland • Brenda Nixon • Dympna Nuree • June O'Connor • Carrielynn Peace • Will Perkins • Angela Pisel • Marilyn Prasow • Naomi Rhodes • Sharon Riddle • Eileen Rife • Mary Beth Robb • Celeste Roberts • Jeneal Rogers • Martha Rogers • Nancy Rose

• Laura Deaton Russell • Mae Frances Sarratt • Joanne Schulte • Joyce Seabolt • Margie Seger • Linda Evans Shepherd • Theresa Sheppard • Shirley Shibley • Ruth Sigmon • Mike Smith • Jim Sweeney • Kathy Thomas • Shirl Thomas • Jan C. Thompson • Charlene Toomey • Erin Torr • Mairin Torr • Shevawn Torr • June Varnum • Stephen Walsh • Claudia Russell Ward • Marion Wells • Kathie Williams • Gary Winters • Brenda Woodard • Mary Yerkes • Jeanne Zornes

Karen O'Connor is a sought-after speaker, a writing consultant, and the award-winning author of more than 75 books, including *Gettin' Old Ain't for Wimps* (more than 400,000 copies sold). She's appeared on national media, including *The 700 Club* and *100 Huntley Street*. Visit her at www.KarenOConnor.com.

To learn more about Harvest House books and
to read sample chapters, visit our website:

www.HarvestHousePublishers.com

HARVEST HOUSE PUBLISHERS
EUGENE, OREGON